The Challenge of Authentic Education

To Diane —
gre
great
buddy!

Great smile!
Love,
Toni

I love those that support
the arts out of a great
love and devotion to
them. Kindred spirit,
Jen

The Challenge of Authentic Education

BOOK ONE:

Joyful Learning in a School Community

by Jay & Toni Garland

Meadowlark Press ❖ Dublin, New Hampshire ❖ 2004

This volume is dedicated to Ursual Garland (our Oma) and our marvelous children: Kambrah, Akhil, and Alexandra. They nourished and sustained us during our thirty-four years of teaching and directing our school. What a team!

Special thanks to Fritz Weatherbee for providing many of the photographs. Others came from the Bauhan, Eldredge and Garland family albums.

Garland, Jay, 1939-
  The challenge of authentic education / Jay and Toni Garland.
     p. cm.
  Includes bibliographical references and index.
  Contents: bk. 1. Joyful learning in a school community
  ISBN 0-87233-135-0 (pbk. : alk. paper)
  1. Education--Philosophy. 2. Alternative education. 3. Well School
(Peterborough, N.H.) I. Garland, Toni, 1938- II. Title.

  LB14.7.G38 2004
  371.04'09742'8--dc22

                        2004001228

Printed in Canada

Meadowlark Press is a division of William L. Bauhan, Inc.,
Dublin, New Hampshire

Meadowlark Press
P.O. Box 34
Portsmouth, NH 03802

Call us toll free: 877-832-3738
or visit our website:
www.themeadowlarkpress.com

Contents

Acknowledgements

We are extremely appreciative to the parents and alumni for sending us on a sabbatical year so that we could complete our book. We thank Kate and Russell Mott and Jan and Ray Cartade for providing a place out west for us to write.

To Martie Majoros, Jonathan Hall, Susan Thompson, Dorothy Verney, and Aaron Garland—your ideas for editing helped bring the book to fruition.

Sarah Bauhan and Joanna Morrissey provided the enthusiasm and support to make publishing a reality. Thank you.

We deeply appreciate the spirit, love, and commitment given by all our students, parents, teachers and friends.

Introduction

Even before we opened the doors to The Well School, it was clear to Toni and me that there was an unseen force at work that was guiding us as we developed the school. It was as if a plan for a new school had already been fully developed, a plan beyond our comprehension, and we were only the custodians of this plan. We understood this to be true throughout our years of involvement as parents, teachers, and directors.

We were always at a loss to adequately describe this creation. Oddly, many parents trusted us implicitly from the start and needed no coherent explanation. Inexplicably, there were families that seemed to have made up their minds to enroll their children even before they met us or had a tour of the campus.

When we developed a brochure explaining the school to prospective Well parents, it was obvious that the true nature of the school could not be put into words or pictures. Parents told us that when they described The Well to friends or relatives, others could not understand what they were talking about. It lay beyond their experience.

It wasn't until we retired that we were able to fully understand and write about our experience at The Well. Only then did we have the perspective to appreciate the scope of our efforts during our thirty-four, very busy years. Yet, rather than having in our possession a series of images that fit together to make up a complete picture, we were left with individual snapshots. But each snapshot offered us a chance to view The Well from a unique perspective.

There are six perspectives that we flesh out in our writing. The sequence may not be important from a reader's point of view as each stands independently on its own. Yet, considered together, they form a complete picture of The Well, based on our experience.

In our first book, *Joyful Learning in a School Community*, we account for the founding and naming of the school. We explain the core principle of Inclusion and describe how it imbued and defined a number of school activities and its importance in establishing a community that consisted of students, parents, and teachers.

A second perspective, *Consciousness as the Key to Learning*, contends that the vitality of a school and the self-discipline of its students depend on the open, honest communication of students and teachers. It addresses the importance of authentic learning that is based on the inner needs of individuals. It promotes education that creates experiences that enable us to know our strengths, address our weaknesses, and widen our perspectives.

The Self as the Center of Learning compares the processes and results of teaching directly to the self, the dynamic center of the personality, with the traditional practice of focusing teaching on the highly restrictive ego. It highlights the use of material with symbolic content that is relevant to the student's individual life path and promotes the expansion of consciousness and the development of inner resources.

Our fourth viewpoint, *The Emergence of Self in Adolescence*, considers the development of Self during puberty and the transition to adolescence. When Horace Mann introduced the compulsory education system, adolescents were barred from work, the apprentice system died, and young Americans were warehoused in schools. This volume focuses on how to give responsibility and a voice back to our youth. We discuss the need for appropriate studies and activities which give teenagers a healthy outlet for their unbridled energy.

Academics for the Heart focuses on alternative curricula and teaching methods that nourish both the mind and the spirit. Recommendations for a general curriculum are explored, with an emphasis on preserving the vitality and open-mindedness natural to children. Materials that encourage self-knowledge, spiritual development, and the need for self-expression in the maturing student form the core of the suggested curriculum.

The sixth volume of the series, *How to Create an Authentic School*, orients parents and teachers to practical methods and approaches for starting and running a small independent school or for homeschooling children. It questions the educational value of teacher certification and details the essential qualities of great teachers.

We now recognize The Well School was, at heart, a homeschool, albeit an elaborate variation of what has become the very popular theme of creating an environment which is built around sharing life together. Originally, our house was the only center of the school, a house with open doors that, from the time we bought the property, have never been locked.

When Toni and I opened our "inner doors" to those first families and their children, we were fully loved in return. At the same time, many parents opened their houses to us. Already we had forged our school community. R.M. and Art Eldredge's studio barn was ours to use for plays, poetry recitals, dances, and get-togethers; it was only a half hour trek through the woods or four miles by circuitous roads. For fifteen years, Carol and Brooks Whitehouse's living room and study allowed space for several reading groups and for many classroom activities. Well School teachers invited their students to their homes for specific activities, for overnights, for a taste of their family life. Tony Brown taught woodworking and carpentry in his spacious shop three miles down the road, and Tony, John Kulish, and Jeff Potter, as well as other teachers, took students beyond the classroom into the woods to study nature.

Because most teachers were also parents of children enrolled at The Well, they trusted and fully supported the distinctive subculture we had created together. Parents attended school events, even ones in which their blood line were not participating. Teachers attended all events, whether their students were involved or not. Boundaries between my children and your children still existed in our personal homes, but not at school. In many ways privacy and secrecy were sacrificed in order to allow an extended intimacy.

Although our classrooms were usually bounded by walls, our classrooms were never isolated. Because the classroom teachers were welcoming, everyone freely visited other classrooms without an invitation or an appointment. Visiting teachers or students were greeted as welcomed guests and often participated in whatever the class was doing. They easily joined in a conversation or tasted some food, just as they would if they were in someone's home.

However, our life together was not an attempt to experience a utopian, casual life style. We came together to create an environment that challenged students to be highly disciplined and responsible, to focus during class, and to be accountable for their significant homework. We were all dedicated to excellence and held ourselves and each other responsible for all our actions. Teachers and students met weekly to share our thoughts and feelings. We informally critiqued each other's attitude, behavior, and work ethic so that we could acknowledge and appreciate individual and group success and resolve any underground resentment that had built up during the week.

To end each day, we all had our designated jobs: cleaning, organizing, and maintaining our environment so that it would be ready for the inevitable tomorrow. At the end of each year, we all cleaned and scrubbed and re-organized until everything was in order for the following year. The teachers, with the help of many parents, then painted all the classrooms and common rooms over a two-day period until we spruced up our environment to be ready for the fall.

There could not have been a professional job description for teachers, for they were asked to do everything, including maintenance of buildings and grounds and the care of the animals. Nor was any job description possible for the students whose responsibilities were extended to match their growth and discipline. Everyone was responsible and pitched in. To us, that's the definition of a healthy home, a healthy community.

Jay and Toni

JAY

Foreword

The only hope for a kind world lies in the ability of man to live in harmony with Nature, to awaken to his true potential, to learn to apprehend and listen to truth, and to unite the inner dimensions of experience with the outer world. For some time, people have been aware that unless mankind abandons its self-destructive path and aligns itself with Spirit, it will perish.

Unless education adopts as its primary goal the nourishment and expression of the inner life of the child, it will continue to sap the life of intuitive, creative children and continue to grind them into a dull, but hostile conformity. Two-and-a-half thousand years ago the sign at Delphi proclaimed, "Know Thyself." Socrates, who put that injunction into practice, created the philosophical basis of Western culture; he inspired a number of disciples, including Plato and Aristotle, whose knowledge dominated the Western World for 1500 years. That age produced life-like sculptures from stone, soaring temples and public buildings, and entire, new fields of endeavor and inquiry: science, history, mathematics, drama, music, and philosophy. It also produced a new experiment in the distribution of political power, democracy.

Socrates challenged the teachers of his day, exposing the ignorance and pretense of sophists. As a result, he was brought to trial, charged with corrupting the youth, and sentenced to death or exile from Athens. He preferred death, drinking hemlock in the company of his friends.

Thousands of others, including Buddha and Christ, also taught the same message: Look within for the source of power, wisdom, health, beauty, harmony, and inspiration.

What follows is an attempt to explain the history and essence of a school we founded in 1967 and left in 2002. Although in so many ways our students speak volumes about the success of the school, we intend here to witness our own remarkable journey of overseeing a school based on the assumption that each child already possesses an inner genius, a spirit of infinite worth, and a capacity for greatness.

The tone is intentionally subjective, rather than professional, because this school arose from a series of subjective experiences as well as from inner prompting. I will focus on a number of personal life experiences, which strongly influenced the direction our school would take. But I will also attempt to persuade the reader that the principle of Community, applied to education, creates a harmonious, joyful environment that animates and promotes accelerated learning.

My hope is that this book will be the first of a series of six which will examine various aspects of education and present what, in our experience, cries out for reform. From our perspective, many possibilities for assisting in the unfolding of compassion, wisdom, and beauty in students lie in the future once educators finally address the fundamental, divine nature of the child.

My life partner, Toni, will present a subjective chronology of the first five years of The Well, beginning in 1967. Her stories are necessary to balance my presentation and to reflect the influence her natural spirituality and optimism had on the development of the school.

Prelude

The heavy-handed pedagogic approach that attempts to fit irrational phenomena into a preconceived rational pattern is anathema to me.
Carl Jung

Life experience is largely irrational. At its deepest level, life defies all logical interpretation and refuses to submit to a rational scheme. And those who, in their driving need for an ordered, circumscribed universe, have fashioned a system of education based on the domestication and control of children to serve corporate ends, have created a monster. Both public and private schooling in America have, in the last century, opted for larger and larger factory-like schools inimical to the human spirit and hostile to input from parents. The utopia envisioned by elite industrialists has, indeed, come to pass, with a terrible fallout: too many students with an impoverished inner life; too many children who can barely read, write, or think; too many impersonal robots who are programmed to listlessly follow directions, work in subservient roles, and prepared to spend themselves into debt in order to acquire the outward trappings of respect.

Without creative personalities able to think and judge independently, the upward development of society is as unthinkable as the development of the individual personality without the nourishing soil of the community.

Albert Einstein

The school that my wife and I created and directed, the school where we taught full-time for thirty-four years, attempted to correct the meaningless education we experienced in our youth by providing a heart-based curriculum in tune with the inner, spiritual (not the religious) needs of each child. In our eyes, The Well School was singularly effective, but rather than present it as a fait accompli, I would first like to present bits of my own personal experience in the hope of revealing aspects of the genesis of The Well.

At an early age, I was tranquilized by an educational system I didn't understand. My earliest memories (before attending school) are of a young boy happily playing with a hose in a small back yard, watching the stream of water puddle and then wind its way under the fence, across the grass, down our driveway of tiny, blue stones, accelerate over a cement pad, turn abruptly left and flow against the curb down our street to a drain where it met a main avenue. My next memory is years later returning from school, lying on my bed, trying to figure out why everyone submitted to school without protest, trying to create some reason or meaning to school's ever-repeated, senseless patterns.

As a young student in the public schools of Mount Vernon, New York, a town which abutted The Bronx, a borough of New York City, I was disconnected and afraid. I missed most of second grade, feeling sick in the morning and recovering remarkably about ten o'clock each day. I lived in dread that I would be locked in the second-grade clothes closet, as a few of my classmates had been. In the spring of that year, I was sent to a special building where I was observed by a host of concerned adults while I played to my heart's delight in a mock-kindergarten observation classroom. The sandbox, the clay, the drawing supplies—I settled into this environment as if it were my personal school. But too soon for my liking the psychologists made their decision: skip Jay to third grade with a new teacher who, they promised, would never lock me in a closet.

In retrospect, my teachers were no doubt competent professionals. But my understanding, as a kid, was that they were adults who were distant, removed, and who owed nobody an explanation of who they were or what they were up to. They might occasionally address me as a person, but it was understood that they were professionals—they owed me nothing. Their personal life was private, inaccessible, and sacrosanct.

It was this legitimized, official aloofness that separated school from the rest of my existence. It lay within the power of the teacher as a masked figure to set up the parameters of the classroom, to determine every activity, and to determine when it would start and end. Teacher as rule maker and orchestrator; teacher as judge of what was fair, what was true, what was right. Teacher as punisher. This figure was so awesome in my mind that I could see no limits to that power. Yet it was inconceivable to question their right to control everything. My teachers may have been kind queens, but I never felt that kindness. Separation was a given, for now and forever. Separation conferred authority, separation created the unreality of my whole school experience.

The value of the creative faculty derives from the fact that faculty is the primary mark of man. To deprive man of its exercise is to reduce him to subhumanity.
Eric Gill

Teaching youngsters isn't much like making steel ... and essential as good technique is, I don't think education is basically a technological problem. It is a problem of drawing out of each youngster the best he has to give and of helping him to see the world he is involved in clearly enough to become himself – among other people – in it, while teaching him the skills he will need in the process.
Edgar Z. Friedenberg

In my time at public school, my classmates never did unite against this menacing power, for we were in competition, striving for some nebulous reward. We never tried to understand our school environment; we never even spoke of it!

Up to that point in my life, social intercourse among all adults was, in my experience, also marked by an element of separation. In my naiveté, I had assumed that at any point each person could discard his role, and reveal, behind his mask, another person, a Wizard of Oz. "Look," the Wizard says, "the mask is off. I'm weak and harmless. I'll never hurt you." That never happened. Even as a five- or six-year-old, I pondered at length the daily drama, looking for the secret of why people never removed their camouflage.

Behind no prison grate, she said, Which slurs the sunshine half a mile, Love captures so uncomforted As soul behind a smile.
Elizabeth Barrett Browning

The barrenness I experienced in my own schooling, coupled with the disconnect from those adults that surrounded me outside school, dominated my early years. My inability to emotionally relate to my school studies and the niggling sense that the deepest truths about life were never even mentioned, made my whole experience of learning surreal. Yes, I performed well on tests, but I might as well have been learning about life on a fictitious planet. To me, the ridiculous life of Dick and Jane and Spot and their generations of descendants were not worth reading about.

Only much later did I realize that what my education lacked was heart and meaning. I recall that at the age of twelve or thirteen I had the strong impression of awakening for the first time from a relentless dream of nothingness. It was as if I had been sleeping for many years and had finally roused myself from my own torpor and despair to discover a living reality within me and about me. I wondered at the marvelous transformation. The past years now appeared to me as one extended dream made up of endless patterns of ugly confusion. But now the old nightmare gave way to clarity and prompted new, burning questions about the nature and significance of all reality.

Five experiences encapsulate that time of waking. The first involved witnessing belief, in particular the nature of Jewish faith and ritual. Almost our whole neighborhood was casually Jewish (my parents, however, were atheists), and my forays into the synagogues with my friends somehow burned me awake. These friends were not orthodox, so I saw little evidence of faith in their homes. In the synagogue, however, there were a few adults who appeared so mesmerized and given to surrender that I figured something mighty must be occurring. I couldn't understand the religious service in Hebrew, but I stayed and watched as I might watch a foreign film with no subtitles. I knew implicitly that I was watching something with meaning. Meaning, humming in my head, brushing against my sides, tickling me. I could somehow sense that in the air was a certain tension or energy that was both new and foreign to me. It attracted me, but I lacked the words to describe it. I knew I didn't belong there. Yet, someone must have given me a lavender yamaka, for I found myself wearing it to synagogue on several occasions.

At that time, I was a student at Wilson Junior High, a school which had a number of students of Christian background. I was wary of Christians with their inflated views of the power of their leader. I remember being very resentful, even jealous, of Jesus, to the point of nursing a hatred for him and deliberately debunking him. Yet, the second of the five most telling experiences of this time was witnessing at school the regular ridicule of a large, awkward boy, Eugene, who unabashedly and convincingly, without presumption, told whoever would listen about his daily conversations with angels. The essence of those conversations was simple and conveyed to me, through its mundane details, a comforting gentleness.

The ugliness which occurred on the playground to make Eugene pay for his crime of belief, the kids' version of poetic justice, did not cause me to intervene, only to watch with a sense of helplessness. Not only was I struck by the overwhelming, relentless cruelty, but also by the absolute absurdity of that cruelty. I did, however, over time, process the message: Direct individual experience of the powers of the invisible world was subject to harsh reprisal. I internalized the message as if I had seen it scrawled in blood on a filthy wall. I would be careful never to expose myself to such ridicule.

The third telling experience was my friendship with two criminal peers, fellow students in eighth grade. They were veterans in crime who invited me to join them. They sat close to me near the back of the classroom. I remember the countdowns as we eyed each other: five, four, three, two, one, and their homemade bomb would detonate on the playground. We celebrated quietly, smugly. Occasionally, I went with them on their rounds of vandalism, shooting out streetlights, breaking windows, running and hiding from the police cars.

> The study of crime begins with the knowledge of oneself. All that you despise, all that you loathe, all that you reject, all that you condemn and seek to convert by punishments springs from you.
>
> **Henry Miller**

I remember riding one-handed on our bikes for five or six miles while holding, in the other hand, wrenches in a bag. Alongside a reservoir in the center of a very public park, we descended some stairs until we were out of view of passers-by. There, in a restricted hole, we managed to turn the controls until we heard below us the sound of water rushing through a culvert. We were thrilled by the idea of emptying a large public water source in broad daylight while people strolled by, some arm and arm, others steering baby carriages, unaware of the scope of our cleverness.

Later, as the three musketeers, we returned to close the gate device, satisfied that the level of the reservoir had dropped significantly. I learned from Bill and Harry that there were interstices between the solid rules of society which one could, with a little daring, navigate. Society did not rule and determine everything as I had feared; one could live outside the dull dream of others.

The fourth experience was a field trip. Our English class went to a performance of Jean Anouilh's *The Lark* in New York City. I remember being deeply stirred by this play which told the story of Joan of Arc. I was stunned and confused, in awe and angry. I needed to clarify what had happened. How did Joan withstand the relentless pressure of the church officials who demanded that she disavow her immediate experience? Was she another Eugene? What impelled her to suffer with dignity the barbarism and conniving of the church authorities? Why were they threatened? Why did she trust her voices? Was she mad, deluded? Or was she the most amazing thing I had ever seen? Was I a fool to be upset by her courage? What courage!

She was precious to me, because, so clearly, she decided with her heart, not her reason; the churchmen's reason made no sense to her. She didn't need to reason. She knew. She was so enthusiastic, even grateful for being asked to make sacrifices for her country. The deadly authority of churchmen meant nothing to her! She was successfully standing alone against the collective reality of others. Wow! Was it not a miracle to respond to fear, hatred, and duplicity with, of all emotions, enthusiasm? She was, however, no martyr, because she lacked a martyr's heaviness and darkness. She was simply dancing light. Something broke open inside of me. I felt I could be courageous if I was devoted to a worthy cause. Perhaps I was not an atheist, as I had supposed. Yet the behavior of the churchmen was repugnant.

The human soul needs actual beauty even more than bread
D.H. Lawrence

When you reach the heart of life you shall find beauty in all things, even the eyes that are blind to beauty.
Kahlil Gibran

The fifth was interacting with my future wife, Toni, every day—in the same class with Bill and Harry—my first real contact with a girl my age. I sat directly behind her in class. When the teacher was not looking, we joked and punched each other a lot. I had no idea that years later we would take on the world together. But we did date and test the waters until my "friend" Bill, told me that Toni no longer wanted to date me, and, being the fool I was, I didn't check out this message with Toni until three years had elapsed. Although this brief period was the first time in my life I remember being completely awake, I don't recall when I went to sleep again, although that sleep lasted for several years.

I woke up again in high school, shocked that I had languished so long in a dream world. My mother gave me a book of modern drama, *Treasury of the Theatre* which housed dozens of incredible plays that boldly expressed viewpoints I could relate to: *RUR* (Karel Capek's precursor to *A Brave New World* involving the use of genetic engineering to make robots), *The Hairy* Ape (Eugene O'Neill's portrayal of industrialized man as a caged animal), *The Emperor Jones* (also by Eugene O'Neill, a play of slavery and the misuse of power), Marc Connelly's *Green Pastures* (a play which portrays God in Heaven reacting in a very human way to the flow of events on earth), Arthur Miller's *Death of a Salesman* (a play which made me nauseous for a week as if I had received a deep and potent blow in my stomach), Jean Anouilh's *The Lark* (allowing me to review the play I had seen in New York), Fredrico Garcia Lorca's *Blood Wedding* (the ultimate passionate lyric tragedy), and dozens more. It was the most meaningful gift I had ever received. I actually began to read without compulsion for the first time in my life, because my hunger for meaning emerged from the darkness and exploded.

It was in high school that I felt my calling must be basketball, because the coach got so excited about my ability to shoot from the perimeter. "Garland," he said, "every time you get the ball, shoot it. You don't

While my hair was still straight across my forehead I played about the front gate pulling flowers. You came by an bamboo stilts, playing horse. You walked about my seat, playing with blue plums. And we went on living in the village of Chokan. Two small people, without dislike or suspicion. At fourteen I married My Lord, you ...
Ezra Pound

Do ye know the terror of him who falleth asleep? To the very toes he is terrified, because the ground giveth away under him, and the dream beginneth.
Friedrich Nietzschc

The true nature of things, truth itself, can be revealed to us only by fantasy, which is more realistic than all the realism. ...Fantasy is revealing; it is a method of cognition: everything that is imagined is true; nothing is true if it is not imagined.
Eugene Ionesco

seem to ever miss." Although I saw myself more as a supporting player as I had been in junior high school, I was persuaded to launch the ball every time I had the opportunity to shoot. His confidence in me was matched by a rising confidence of my own, based on a sweet feeling to which I was becoming addicted.

Basketball took on an added dimension late in the season. An opposing player who felt I had taken too many rebounds from him threatened retribution after the game. I laughed it off. But in our locker room before going home, Bobby Lennox, our cocky black guard, said he would be my body guard and opened his gym shorts to reveal a knife he had worn throughout the game.

The threatening and posturing after the game in the parking lot came to nought, but I was flattered that my white ass was worth fighting for. I was apparently, for all my reckless shooting, part of a team. Sweet again. Basketball had a lot to offer. It had no real meaning, but it was safe!

But after my sophomore season, my basketball days were over. My mother's concern about my tremor which showed as a involuntary trembling of my hands, led her to take me to a neurologist in New York City. I tried to dismiss the doctor's serious demeanor as he repeatedly looked into my eyes with a little, blue, metallic flashlight, giving me orders on where to focus. When I failed his cup and saucer test, unable to keep them quiet, the doctor muttered and nodded.

He asked my mother for a private conference which was over before I anticipated what it could possibly mean. The announcement, "No more basketball," froze me. Outside the office, I demanded an explanation from my mother. What could be the possible connection between a rattling cup and saucer and basketball. He never even saw me play. My mother could not explain, but she was unwilling to defy the authority of the doctor. I thought long and hard on how decisions were made, but I came up with nothing that made sense. I did, however, accept that basketball was not part of my destiny after all.

Whenever I watch a basketball game in person or on a television screen, I return to the dream of my youth and partake. One part of my being coaches out loud; other parts shoot and pass and rebound the ball. At such times, my heart rate increases, almost as if my own future were on the line. Even bouncing a ball awakens the sleeping vision.

Prospects in the classroom, however, improved. I recall in geometry class, my teacher struggling to explain Euclidean proofs to most of the students. I volunteered to solve problems whose solutions seemed obvious. She had the grace to have me, thereafter, explain most of the proofs. I worked extra hard on my homework, not just to get a proof, but to get it well enough to explain it to someone who hadn't a clue where to begin. I wanted to show, beyond a doubt, how the solutions were present in the problems themselves. In time, I measured myself against the standard of solving every problem. It set me up and motivated me, as I see now, for a career in teaching.

Another academic teacher who captured my attention and furthered my development was my American History teacher. Mr. McKearney, despite the fact that he taught by the book from an excessively patriotic boring text (I yearned for the concrete details of each event), revealed his human-ness as well as his humaneness. He was so anxious that we, as students, related to the material; his passion for history was obvious. Knowing that our grades on exams were interpreted by Mr. McKearney as his own personal report card, I wanted to do well for him more than myself. He caught me cheating on the test and quietly let me know, docking my grade appropriately. Although the initial shame was intense, I soon understood that I was totally forgiven by him. How odd! I was the proverbial prodigal son, forgiven by a father who loved me. Could I be a prodigal son if I was ambivalent about God?

I had seriously considered not going to college in order to escape the academic world which, for the most part, deadened me. My mother, however, had arranged, without my knowledge, for my half-brother, Peter, to give me a tour of his alma mater, Harvard College. I reluctantly met Peter in Cambridge. Inwardly, I was unenthusiastic about the school, but I was heartened at being connected with a brother I didn't know. (Peter was the oldest of ten children from two marriages and two affairs on my father's side, and I was the youngest). As it turned out, Harvard was the only college I applied to, and the day I was accepted, I invited Mr. McKearney to our house to have a glass of wine with my family. Ambivalent as I was toward the prospect of college, I knew that Mr. McKearney needed to be there. He was the only teacher to ever come through the door of our house. I loved him.

Toni and I reconnected during my senior year in high school and developed a close connection that would withstand the separation occasioned by college. We became best friends before we became lovers, earning each others respect in a partnership that, in many ways, resembled a brother/sister relationship that I never had with my own sisters. I had no need to be defensive in her presence as I was with others. I was free! Her joy and passion for the simplest of life experiences lifted me, calmed me, and enchanted me. How could she be unconcerned how others judged her? Why was I so concerned? Did she and Joan of Arc share some secret?

Harvard College, that venerable pillar of western learning, should have marked the educational high point of my life. Instead, I found that Harvard, in many ways, mocked life. True, I was poorly prepared for the academic rigors of Harvard, unable to write a simple, coherent essay and unpracticed in critical reading. Oh, the initial three weeks as a freshman stimulated me as I had never been stimulated before, because I discussed with my new acquaintances such a variety of ideas, and there seemed to be so many wonderful possibilities to consider.

It is the rigid dogma that destroys truth; and, please notice, my emphasis is not on the dogma but on the rigidity. We men say of any question,"This is all there is to be known or said of the subject; investigation ends here," that is death.

Alfred North Whitehead

I have grown to believe that the one thing worth aiming at is simplicity of heart and life; that one's relation with others should be direct and not diplomatic; that power leaves a bitter taste in the mouth; that meanness, and hardness, and coldness are the unforgivable sins; that conventionality is the mother of dreariness; that pleasure exists not in virtue of material conditions, but in the joyful heart; that the world is a very interesting and beautiful place; that congenial labour is the secret of happiness; and many other things that seem, as I write them down, to be dull and trite commonplaces, but are for me the bright jewels which I have found beside the way.

A.C. Benson

As I saw other students, one by one, settle into a routine of daily study, I felt abandoned. I felt more lonesome and alienated than ever before. I envied their ability to commit to academic rigors; on the other hand, I judged and condemned them as sheep. I would look out my window each evening at the figures, seated at study in the windows of neighboring dormitories across the lawn, and weep uncontrollably for those who forsook inquiry for the sake of study. Who was the fool, them or me?

My own classes, especially in my freshman year, were abysmal and, to me, utterly humiliating. To have a teacher read his book on anthropology over the course of weeks and months, out loud, without interruption, while three hundred students took notes, or slept, offended my dignity and intelligence. To have another teacher reject out of hand my questions about other ways of looking at a subject, as if I were a fly which had landed on his jelly doughnut, made me feel invisible. (I spin into an inner frenzy when ignored.) To have a philosophy professor lecture endlessly about what was wrong with Plato, Aristotle, Hegel, Hume and Kant as if his superior mind could hardly fathom how these beginners could make such elementary errors in thinking, made me sick. I felt battered, listening to his superior, belittling tone, a tone which I soon began to identify with all of Harvard. Didn't everyone there imitate that tone? Was no one awed by what they were teaching? Could no one admit to the impenetrable mystery of life? Wasn't life a mystery? Why, when I visited my childhood friend at Brandeis, did everyone seem so accepting and refreshing?

I felt that if anyone on earth could understand my emptiness, it would be my father, a mild, understanding man who, himself, had fled Harvard after a year of frustration there. We arranged to meet in Cambridge, and, over a meal in a Chinese restaurant on Church Street, we talked—or rather, I talked—into the night until I was exhausted. I assumed my father had been listening intently, and I waited for his decisive reply. When he responded, "I'm kind of tired, Jay, and I'm afraid I haven't been taking anything in," I went into a state of shock that lasted for some months. I was completely undone, totally alone.

A week later, after cramming all night on No-Doze, I took my first semester exam at Memorial Hall . After the exam, crossing the street, I found myself floating above the ground as the driver of a sixteen-wheeler leaned out the window of his cab and screamed vulgarities at

The Mystery of Pain

Pain has an element of blank;
It cannot recollect
When it began, or if there were
A day when it was not.

It has no future but itself,
Its infinite realms contain
Its past, enlightened to perceive
New periods of pain.

Emily Dickinson

30

Much madness is divinest sense
To a discerning eye;
Much sense the starkest madness
'T is the majority
In this, as all, prevails.
Assent, and you are sane:
Demur, – you're straightway dangerous,
And handled with a chain.

Emily Dickinson

Sympathy

I know what the caged bird feels, alas!
    When the sun is bright on the upland slopes;
When the wind stirs soft through the springing grass
And the river flows like a stream of glass;
    When the first bird sings and the first bud opes,
    And the faint perfume from its chalice steals –
I know what the caged bird feels!

I know why the caged bird beats his wing
    Till blood is red on the cruel bars;
For he must fly back to his perch and cling
When he fain would be on the bough a-swing;
    And a pain still throbs in the old, old scars
    And they pulse again with a keener sting –
I know why he beats his wing!

I know why the caged bird sings, ah me,
    When his wing is bruised and his bosom sore,--
When he beats his bars and would be free;
It is not a carol of joy or glee,
    But a prayer that he sends from his heart's deep core,
    But a plea that upward to Heaven he flings—
I know why the caged bird sings.

Paul Lawrence Dunbar

me. I was, it seems, suspended on the front of his truck, but basically I was unharmed. Once I was safely across Cambridge Avenue, I found it painful to breathe the cold air. I threaded my way back to my dorm through a number of buildings, oblivious of what function they served, aware only that they held heat. I climbed to the fifth floor of Matthews, my dorm, and collapsed, unconscious, in front of my unopened door.

I awoke in the Harvard infirmary where I remained for three weeks. For all their medical tests, the doctors could not diagnose what ailed me. But, for me, my temporary home was perfect for contemplating what had happened to me. I felt lost. Perhaps I was crazy; mental illness was rampant in my family. I read strange novels set in the East, in which some sadist tortured others unmercifully for the sheer fun it gave him. I could relate well to the victim, but I realized then that my case could be far worse. I was in no physical pain!

Soon after being discharged, I had a number of prolonged out-of-body experiences (sometimes all day) without ever using mind-altering drugs. My center of consciousness floated just behind and above the left side of my body, and from there, I could watch my body and everything else in front of me. During these periods, I experienced, for the first time in my life, a sense of total security and invulnerability, and subsequently, total relaxation. The relief was sublime! I was disconnetced from my ego, but connetced to a higher power! For several nights running, unable to believe my luck, I walked across traffic in Harvard Square with my eyes closed to test the veracity of my new sense of power. It worked as if I had been a naked American Indian counting coup on palefaces while bullets whizzed about my magically protected body.

I had not only survived a period of painful isolation while in the midst of thousands of others who were being initiated into the elite class of our society, but I had also grown more powerful in the process. Their world, I decided, had nothing to do with my reality. Why compare my lot with theirs?

And my reading of novels during my convalescence had, in a warped way, opened a doorway to the East. Fortuitously, I found, in a bookstore on Massachusetts Avenue in Cambridge, amazing books on a variety of Eastern religions. They provided the basis for a strange, but much more plausible, reality which supported me in my quest for some measure of sanity grounded on my individual experience. I realized I was searching for a spiritual identity.

In the spring of my freshman year, I did something totally against my shy nature. I saw a young man walking across a room in a pizza parlor. Something clicked. I crossed the room, introduced myself, and asked if I could talk to him later that night.

Snick Wilson and I became fast friends. I was awed by him; it seems his prep school experience at Exeter had informed him about a number of fields of knowledge I knew nothing about. He could write and read, and he possessed the rudiments of the classical education I had never received. For more than a year, we talked and wrote our own poetry and plays at night, and, after consuming a full breakfast, slept through each day. One thing must be said in Harvard's favor: It was fine to skip classes as long as you showed up for the final exams.

But, as I examine it now, I was obviously not entirely comfortable with the arrangement. For the next fifteen years, many of my dreams dealt with trying to find my way through a maze of hallways, only to end up (in a frantic state) in what seemed to be the wrong classroom or the wrong testing room. When asked by strangers in the dream what class I had signed up for, or what room I was looking for, I could not remember, and humiliated, I would beat a fast retreat and continue my search in other hallways, in other buildings with different, yet similar, mazes.

Individualism is a fatal poison. But individuality is the salt of the common life. You may have to live in a crowd, but you do not have to like it, nor subsist on its food. You may have your own orchard. You may drink at a hidden spring. Be yourself if you would like to serve others.

Henry Van Dyke

After freshman year, as luck would have it, I was assigned to Lowell House, the snobbiest residence of the Harvard house system; the supreme tradition there was high table. No spirit could dwell in this wasteland. Some authority had decided it was to be my home for the rest of my college experience.

But that year, at nineteen, I escaped from this prison into an amazing marriage with Toni. We impulsively wed during her short visit to Harvard, which meant moving off campus. Suddenly I experienced a flood of happiness and a strong sense of security. I felt relieved associating with the ordinary people in our apartment building, an unpretentious battered structure on Harvard Street with a sign nailed to its exterior, "Live and Dead Storage." It was our second home. At the time of our marriage, we had spent a hilarious week in a rooming house principally for elderly people, but we had been evicted because we supposedly woke people in the middle of the night by flushing the toilet. Toni then transferred from Michigan State to Boston University and we both managed, in the end, to graduate.

I was especially interested in studying psychology and took two courses—Yes, I attended classes again; it fit my new, more normal life style—which focused on Freudian theory. I wanted to study the more inspirational Carl Jung, but Harvard was obsessed with Freud, Freud, Freud, Freud! Perhaps they had never heard of Jung. Freud, although very stimulating and exciting, for all his apparent knowledge, seemed ignorant of the spiritual forces I could not escape. No wonder, for in his *Future of an Illusion*, he mocks spirit. Jung, on the other hand, embraced the spiritual self.

At Harvard, I yearned for contact with my teachers. In 1959, I met a professor of psychology, Richard Alpert, who affected the course of the rest of my life. We took several field trips together which included visiting the hell-hole of a mental facility in Laconia, New Hampshire (I could not stomach the horrible images I saw there), and a Waldorf school in Manhattan. The former persuaded me, whatever my circumstances, to avoid, at all costs, mental institutions; the latter whetted my appetite for education. Although I was unmoved by visiting grades two through eight, I was inspired by the tone of a first grade classroom. Even though the students were speaking German, which I did not understand, something invisible called to me. I knew I had found a pearl of great value. (Two years later I would read so much of Rudolph Steiner, who inspired the Waldorf movement, that I overdosed on his many abstractions, and could not read him again. Nevertheless, I did use, at a later date, many of his ideas in my own teaching.)

Dick Alpert became friends with Toni and me. For me, he represented the human side of the psychology department. B.F. Skinner's study of rats in order to learn to control rat behavior and the behavior of humans was repulsive to me. And the strict and blind adherence to Freud as the sole authority on the dynamics of the human mind made me roll my eyes in disbelief.

But Dick's interest in life, in inquiry, and in knowledge, especially when directed in my direction, awakened me to the positive aspects of college. When we discussed, among other topics, the psychological implications of my out-of-body experiences of my freshman year and his life as the son of a railroad magnate, I knew I was talking to someone who knew he didn't have all the answers. Our trip to Manhattan to explore a school was in response to my personal interest in trying to figure out my life, in general, and my education, in particular. Dick's interest in me as a person opened a door for me into the field of education.

Subsequently, I learned that he, along with Timothy Leary, had been fired for giving drugs to college students as part of their experimentation with mind-altering substances, but the topic never came up between us.

But Dick Alpert's influence led me to write a prospectus for a new school which, in my imagination, provided the kind of learning I had longed for. The school was just a chimera. I had no intention of putting into practice what seemed only a personal fantasy. But my friend Snick was relentless in forcing me to realize I could be involved in such a school.

Then another friend, Rick, who seemed to have his finger on all the relevant information in the universe, gave me the address of the Bureau of Indian Affairs in Juneau, Alaska, and told me they were looking for teachers to teach Native Americans. Perhaps I could fit in with the Eskimos. Toni and I quickly filled out applications and sent them to the Bureau.

The Bureau was very encouraging, except it let us know that twenty-four hours of education credits were required before the jobs started in September. Although Toni already met the requirement, I had, at that time, zero credit hours in education. So, in my last semester, I took two education courses at Harvard, eight credits at Boston University, and eight at the State Teachers College in Boston. These education courses were uninspiring at the time and in retrospect, utterly useless and often degrading. The credits, however, served my purpose.

Conditionally, we were hired to teach at Barrow, Alaska, on the Arctic Ocean, the northernmost settlement and the largest Eskimo community in the United States. We made out our order for a year's worth of groceries to be shipped in before the "freeze-up," then put our belongings into a huge crate which would be shipped with our groceries to Barrow. The adventure of our new life had finally begun in earnest.

When we actually began teaching in Barrow, it was obvious that the books which were provided to teach reading were a total turnoff to students. The story about dad coming home, newspaper under arm, greeting Spot and the children was ridiculous. It did not relate to anything in the village. Dad never came home with the newspaper, and Spot was part of a snarling, smelly, dog sled team chained near the house. The stories in the readers were inane for kids in modern cities, let alone Eskimos in the wilderness. I looked for other kinds of reading at the school, but there was nothing, in my view, appropriate. Perhaps we could focus on writing instead of reading. We did publish what Eskimo stories the kids could find, that were part of the community's oral tradition, but there were only a few elderly people who knew those stories. The project could not be sustained.

I decided to use Greek myths and ordered by mail, without permission, enough copies for my class. If mythology had universal appeal, these books would work. It was worth a try. I told my class I had ordered some books specifically for them and they were excited. When Robert Graves' *Greek Gods and Heroes* arrived, the books looked beautiful to me. The first few minutes we read together out loud, my faith in mythology was restored, and I got a strong jolt of confidence as a new teacher. The students appreciated the stories immediately. It allowed us to discuss some of the complexities of human nature and to be able to compare the experiences of Graves' gods and heroes with our own experiences. We read about the twelve Olympian gods; the underworld of Tartarus, the birth of Hermes, Demeter and the loss of her daughter, Persephone, Orpheus and Eurydice, the healer Asclepius, Theseus, Heracles, Jason and the Golden Fleece, and others. We read most of these stories out loud because of the limited vocabulary of the students. Our discussions spurred great interest in the class. I thought it a great success.

Before we arrived in Barrow, there had been very little visiting outside of class between students and teachers. There was even a rule forbidding teachers to visit Eskimo homes. Fortunately, with the new principal, all that changed for us. Three lively girls often visited Toni and me in our apartment, making many batches of cookies, giggling, and talking a lot. I may not remember or spell their names correctly, but what I recall is Martha Jane Aikens, Beverly Nusunginya , and Flossie Hopson. They loved writing the newspaper we printed. Their faces, if not their names, are etched in my memory. Their responsive nature made me fall in love with teaching children. Perhaps I had found my calling. I am indebted to their influence on me.

In our first year at Barrow, Toni and I lived adjacent to our new principal, John Gordon, his wife, Wilma, and their kids. John and Wilma immediately included us in their life. John had access to a Jeep and often invited me, as his buddy, to go with him on his rounds of

The great desideratum of human education is to make all men aware that they are gods in the making, and that they can all walk upon water if they will.

Don Marquis

government agencies: the weather station, the DEW line (Distant Early Warning system guarding against incursions of the Russian military), and the Bureau of Weights and Standards. Then we would return to town and visit the pool hall, the government hospital, the post office, the store, and the hotel. On these trips, John often told stories that I knew were untrue, i.e. "We just came from the airport where Benson told me he would arrange to send me some new sound equipment," or "Jennings said he'd get me a new set of tires for nothing." The stories, if daring, were harmless, but I tried to persuade John to give them up. In my own mind, as I realized later, I was very judgmental toward him for the lies he told and, consequently, always uneasy in his presence, friendly and generous though he was to me.

Our second year, we managed to move to an older, dilapidated apartment in another building, which was a relief. For me, the event of the year was the birth of our daughter, Kambrah, on the first day of spring. Toni and I had a new wonder in our life together which reminded us daily how lucky we were. I didn't understand it, but the love Kambrah brought with her "from the stars" was new and unconditional.

But near the end of year two when our two-year contract would expire, John asked us to stay in Barrow with him and his family. I was still feeling pressed by my own judgements about his compulsive lying. When I indicated our wish to move to another village, he said, with the wide, winning smile he often wore, he would have to block that request. I felt cornered. So at the end of the year, despite our strong connection to people in Barrow, we resigned from the Bureau of Indian Affairs and returned to New Hampshire. Self-righteously, I refused to be any man's lackey. I see now I was only running away from life. Since I had not faced my own habit of judging others, I was destined to repeat the experience a few years later.

Toni and I looked at schools in the Northeast. The North Country School in Lake Placid, New York, took my breath away, because it resembled so closely what I had described in the prospectus I had written in college. I felt crestfallen. "My God, it's been done already!" Toni, however, was not particularly impressed by the school, and we next visited The Bement School in Deerfield, Massachusetts. Finding it friendly and agreeable to both of us, Toni and I accepted teaching positions there. Toni taught reading with another teacher, and I became the sixth-grade classroom teacher.

After I thought I had adjusted to the boarding school routine, life knocked again. I awakened late one night to find a ball of light floating just above the foot of my bed. I was shocked and frightened at first, but the sense of peace and love which radiated throughout the room, and which I inhaled deeply, overwhelmed me. Spirit had awakened me again! I bathed in the aura for hours, grateful that the invisible was made visible. The second and third night I awoke to exactly the same phenomenon. I relished the nightly visits, for never had I felt such peace and acceptance. Never had I felt so connected to the entire universe. I would never again ignore the presence of spirit in my life!

I told no one, not even Toni. But after three nights of the welcome light, daylight disclosed a greater wonder. During class, a student asked if he could speak to me privately. He revealed that a ball of light had appeared in his room at night and awakened him. He wanted me to tell him what it was. I panicked. I tried to quietly reassure him, but perversity entered. The figures of Eugene and Joan, tortured by idiots masquerading as humans, sprang to mind. I deliberately underplayed the inexplicable event, hoping to avoid any conflict whatever.

But when the very next day, another boy in my class asked for a private chat, I freaked out. I don't even recall our conversation about the appearance of a ball of light, but I recall asking the universe to take away the light. I wanted it understood by whatever power that lay behind the scenes that I wouldn't tolerate any more irregular light in my life!

It startled me then, and it has startled me every time I think of that blessed time, how I underwent a swift spiritual death, because I was unwilling to give voice to my own connection with divinity. I know I failed both those boys, but I failed myself as well. (This is my perversity: denying what is clearly demonstrated to self because it does not conform to the beliefs of others.) In that moment of denial, I died again. I put these disturbing events out of my mind because I had disgraced myself so completely. It was one of the worst things I have ever done. Yet, I felt no shame at the time; I had resolutely chosen death just when I had been given Life. I was left with my numbness. Education could not be my real calling.

Toni bore our second child while we were teaching at the Bement School. Amazingly, our love expanded and grew with our first boy, Akhil. Kambrah was so thrilled to have a brother that she also took special care of him. Family life would sustain me.

But by the end of our second year at Bement, I was restless; I yearned to return to Alaska. We reapplied to the Bureau of Indian Affairs, and near the end of our stay at Bement, we were informed of our new positions as principal and teachers at Pilot Station, an isolated village on the Yukon River, with a population of about two hundred natives. But a shock registered when it was revealed that our new overseer would be John Gordon, now the regional administrator for scores of government schools for Native Americans in southwestern Alaska. How strange is life? Was I just a fly in John's web? Nevertheless, we packed our most precious possessions, choosing this time, only what we thought we could not live without.

While our small plane landed on the Yukon River, we surveyed the village of Pilot Station, snuggled between hills and the wide expanse of the river. The school janitor met us with his boat and took us up a small slough to a landing just behind the school house and presented us with a load of fish for our evening meal. This warm greeting introduced us to the generosity of the people we soon came to love.

The Eskimos in this isolated outpost (weather permitting, small planes landed, once a week, either on the Yukon River or on the airfield atop a nearby hill) were the most hospitable people I have ever known. The rampant alcoholism did not diminish their humanity and generosity. Every home was open to us, and our children were their children. Never have I experienced more inquisitive students, although their homes were occasionally places of violence. These children were absolutely beautiful until about the age of eighteen when, according to some unwritten yet potent rule, many, especially the girls, lost the light in their eyes and walked slumped over like they were the walking dead, without expression or delight, in stark contrast with the younger kids who were totally animated.

Because our family lived in a school house, Kambrah and Akhil were only a few steps away from our classrooms. Home and school were almost one as students dropped in and out of our home. Kambrah, age three, quickly became the darling of many of the families in the village. She never lacked for playmates. On the weekends, she visited her friends and was invited into most of the houses. Her favorite friend, Rosie, lived in a log structure a minute's walk from the school building.

One day I was asked to rush to Rosie's house. There on the floor was Rosie's body, and her upset parents told me that while playing with a boy by the bank of the Yukon River, Rosie had been pushed, and had fallen in. Rosie's only response to our attempts at CPR was to vomit out her stomach contents. We could not revive her. Despite the tragedy at hand, I could not help thinking of what Kambrah's reaction would be. From the way Kambrah had often talked about Rosie, I could sense how much our daughter had depended on Rosie's leadership and friendship. To Toni's and my amazement, Kambrah, though very disappointed to lose a friend, was untroubled by her death. The next day Kambrah stood, uncomplaining, through the three-hour service for Rosie at the Russian Orthodox church and was one of the first to toss some dirt into her grave. She never complained of losing her friend and never doubted that Rosie lived in another dimension of reality. I understood then, that Kambrah, though only three, was one of my teachers. Countless times since then, I have followed her advice—and benefitted from it.

When Toni's mother came to visit us in Pilot Station, her plane also landed on the river. There was always a general stir when a plane was about to arrive. Most of the villagers showed up to greet the plane on the river bank. We were all anxious to meet "Grandma." But when Grandma stepped out of the plane, Kambrah was stunned, almost undone. "Ahh zaa," Kambrah blurted out. "Grandma's a gussuck." "Gussuck" translates as white person. Kambrah, who assumed that our family was Eskimo, could hardly believe her grandmother was not, but she recovered enough to give her a warm hug.

It was at Pilot Station that I began the ritual of telling stories to our children. If the story was before bedtime, Ak would be playing with his blocks, but listening as intently as Kambrah. I found I could communicate well with my children, indirectly, by telling stories, for I could use the symbolic language of fairy tales and myths to talk to them about anything, especially to explain to them that life is about working with the forces of nature and of oneself to meet and overcome all the challenges that come one's way.

We opened a night school to give the kids a place to be in the evening. Attendance was almost the same as in the day session—nearly one hundred percent. Even a seventh-grade girl who had never spoken a word in all her years in school showed up. Interestingly, the students were as motivated to learn each night as they were during the daytime.

By day, Toni taught grades one through four; I taught grades five through eight. We cooked and served students our midday meal. We served as village nurses (with penicillin stored in our ice box) and using the school's short wave radio, we presented cases to doctors in Bethel, Alaska. We received, in return, instructions on how to treat our patients. We sewed up wounds from drunken brawls, gave hundreds of injections, and listened to stories, some of them unbelievably tragic. Yet, we ourselves were loved as we had never been loved; we were safe in a magic land.

When John Gordon visited to see how our school was going, I walked on eggs, afraid again to expose my judgment and fear of him, which had inexplicably not subsided, but grown. We requested that John hire some villagers who knew the Eskimo language to help with the teaching of the youngest kids. He reciprocated, and the school expanded into the Community Hall with help from two native women, Martina and Susie, who lived in the village. Perhaps John and I had accomodated our differences.

The Eskimo community that we experienced became a new family for us. Everyone was always included. At Pilot Station, the Yukon River was almost a mile wide. In the spring of 1965, ice jams hindered the flow of water, and the Yukon rose, overflowed its banks, and spread into the village itself, turning walkways into rafts and lifting log houses off their bases. The flood caused some inconveniences, but it also caused much excitement and joy. Later, after the waters receded, wide sandbars were exposed beside the river.

There, on those sandbars on a warm day, Eskimo children played their strange version of baseball. The pitcher stands next to the batter and throws the ball straight up into the air. The batter is allowed one swing. But whether he hits the ball or not, the batter may run some fifty yards across a danger zone where he can be hit by a ball thrown by somebody whose team is in the field. If he avoids being hit and reaches the safety zone, he may rest before attempting to return in order to earn the right to bat again. If he is hit in the danger zone he may quickly retrieve the ball and hit one of the fielders scrambling for safety at either end of the danger zone. Within seconds, the batters may become fielders and become batters again. There is great joy in the melee; no runs are counted, no winner declared. For me, this precious picture captures the essence of inclusion; you are free to join, free to drop out and join something else; adults and children have the same status; there are no adults organizing things, no signing up for a team, no referees. Everyone wins because there is no arguing or blaming, just laughing. Everyone is included.

One morning, during the long winter of our first year at Pilot Station, I felt a strong interior pain and a shortness of breath that prevented me from either lying down or fully sitting up. Toni radioed a doctor, as well as John Gordon. A nasty front was threatening the local Yukon area, but John arranged to send a pilot out just ahead of the storm. I was bundled up, strapped into a dog sled, taken up the hill to the airfield, and lifted onto the plane which was on the ground for only a minute or two. The pilot and I flew in silence along the seam of a cobalt and ebony sky. When admitted to the hospital, I was thoroughly exhausted and unable to answer questions. I understood that the doctors and nurses took me for an Eskimo who, as they presumed, had been found in a snowbank, drunk.

I awoke to find myself in a Quonset hut which visibly shook from the violence of the storm. I was vomiting all over a large black nurse who was assisting me, then cleaning me up. I stayed awake the rest of the night, at first consciously facing death as an immediate possibility, then, weeping uncontrollably and forgiving John, the man whom I had so heavily judged, the man who had always been the truest of friends to me, then knowing with certitude, even if I was an ingrate, that I was well. Then daylight. John visited me daily.

A week later, John flew Toni and the kids to Bethel to stay with his family and to visit me. My lungs were full of liquid and penicillin brought no relief. The doctors saw death in me and debated whether to send me to Seattle. They tortured me for hours on end, sitting me up, trying to extract fluid through a long needle inserted through my back and into my lungs. For days, dour priests and ministers visited to hear confessions and to give me comfort. I knew I was totally well, but when Toni or John visited, I could see they were deeply worried. I couldn't convince them all was well.

Apparently, the day after I went into the hospital, John had sent a plane to the mouth of the Yukon to search for our belongings, that we had shipped to Alaska. They had been spotted by an airplane pilot, floating in the Bering Sea after the storm subsided. Because of an early "freeze-up" of the Yukon River that fall, our crated personal goods had been dropped on a sandbar at the mouth of the river to be retrieved at some later date. In the storm, the sea had adopted our crate. A pilot, commissioned by John to locate the crate, spotted something bobbing in the sea, but our belongings were never recovered. The loss felt just right, even wonderful, a great relief, part of my recovery.

I understood the nature of my sickness. My condition was just a manifestation of my rigidity and hatred toward a man who had, in every way, acted as one of my angels in life. I interpreted my involuntary forgiveness of John during the night as another intervention of divine light. I was relieved to have my hatred and judgment end, but my forgiveness did not result from any conscious choice of my own. I was a most reluctant learner who still had to be driven to accept goodness freely given. Yet, I was laughing inside like never before.

For still in mutual sufferance lies
The secret of true living;
Love scarce is love that never knows
The sweetness of forgiving.
John Greenlef Whitier

Nevertheless, I could not get beyond working for the Bureau of Indian Affairs. Our teaching, our whole life was wonderful. Even working for John was now comfortable, and I felt great gratitude. But the ultimate mission of the Bureau, which John had showed me in a Bureau of Indian Affairs manual while we were still in Barrow, was to eliminate Native American culture and to move people from remote Alaskan settlements to huge cities like Seattle, Chicago, and Los Angeles. "Relocation," as they called it, was to be preceded by a month or two of training at a trade as a carpenter, a plumber, a painter, etc. The Bureau called the whole process "acculturation." As they saw it, there was no good financial reason to support these remote villagers who would never outgrow their dependence on government assistance, and there was no reason to accommodate or tolerate their culture.

Toni and I then attended a teachers convention for Bureau teachers in Anchorage that confirmed our suspicions about the net effect of the Bureau on natives. I don't remember a word of what was presented at the feel-good convention, but I vividly recall the prevailing attitude of most Bureau teachers: Eskimos are dirty, inferior people that "we" would never associate with if our livelihoods did not depend on it.

44

The combination of fellow teachers' attitudes, bureau policy, and an irrelevant prescribed curriculum we could not always dodge led us to leave the Bureau. We were considering, at the time, going to school in England to study the Waldorf School principles of teaching or teaching on a South Pacific island, when we received a letter from my brother, Peter, another angel-in-the-flesh of mine, imploring us to start a school in New Hampshire. His five children were not enjoying school, and he knew a few other families who wanted to try an alternative model of education.

We never know how high we are
Till we are called to rise;
And then, if we are true to plan,
Our statues touch the skies!

The heroism we recite
Would be a daily thing,
Did not ourselves the cubits wary
For fear to be a king.
Emily Dickinson

After committing to start our own school in Peterborough, New Hampshire, in 1967, we left our beloved Alaska, where we had been so enlivened by teaching Eskimo children in Barrow and Pilot Station. We hoped to incorporate into our new school the wonderful aspects of the Eskimo communities in which we had lived, as well as a multitude of other ideas we derived from our experiences and from our reading. We left Alaska in June of 1967.

Our reception in New Hampshire went well. Parents were willing to entrust us with the education of their children and to allow us to determine what was taught. But we were at odds with what to name our school. Often, when Toni and I experience prolonged or poignant discord with each other and face what seems to be an insurmountable obstacle in our lives together, we turn to a book of ancient Chinese divination called the *I Ching* with the understanding that we agree to do whatever it suggests.

Ching, The Well

In the summer of 1967, we made what was to be a crucial decision. We again consulted the *I Ching* or *Book of Changes* to save us from our frustration. The result was not only a school name, but also, as it turned out, the core of our school. By the toss of coins we were directed to hexagram 48, Ching/The Well, the pole and bucket well of ancient China.[1]

(We were very proud of the new name for our school. But throughout that summer of 1967, New Hampshire was experiencing a severe drought. Well drillers could not keep up with the demand for new wells or the re-drilling of old wells in search of fresh water. Some of our friends were upset with the name we took from the *I Ching* for they associated wells with crippling debt or the continual need to shower.)

I present the main description of The Well in its entirety, because, as a whole, it has silently governed our school over the thirty-four years we directed and taught there.

This hexagram is composed of two groups of three lines, that is, two trigrams. The trigram wood lies above and water lies below. The image is a common plant which gains its nourishment by absorbing water and lifting it to every plant cell.

Ching/The Well

> "Wood is below, water above. The wood goes down into the earth to bring up water. The image derives from the pole-and-bucket well of ancient China. The wood represents not the buckets, which in ancient times were made of clay, but rather the wooden poles by which the water is hauled up from the well. The image also refers to the world of plants, which lift water out of the earth by means of their fibers.

The well from which the water is drawn conveys the further idea of an inexhaustible dispensing of nourishment.

> The Judgment.
> The Well. The town may be changed,
>   But the well cannot be changed.
>   It neither decreases nor increases.
>   They come and go and draw from the well.
>   If one gets down almost to the water
>   And the rope does not go all the way,
>   Or the jug breaks, it brings misfortune.

In ancient China the capital cities were sometime moved, partly for the sake of more favorable location, partly because of a change in dynasties. The style of architecture changed in the course of centuries, but the shape of the well has remained the same from ancient times to this day. Thus the well is the symbol of that social structure which, evolved by mankind in meeting its most primitive needs, is independent of all political forms. Political structures change, as do nations, but the life of man with its needs remains eternally the same—this cannot be changed. Life is also inexhaustible. It grows neither less nor more; it exists for one and for all. The generations come and go, and all enjoy life in its inexhaustible abundance.

However, there are two prerequisites for a satisfactory political or social organization of mankind. We must go down to the very foundations of life. For any merely superficial ordering of life that leaves its deepest needs unsatisfied is as ineffectual as if no attempt at order had ever been made. Carelessness—by which the jug is broken—is also disastrous. If for instance the military defense of a state is carried to such excess that it provokes wars by which the power of the state is annihilated, this is a breaking of the jug.

This hexagram applies also to the individual. And every human being can draw in the course of his education from the inexhaustible wellspring of the divine in man's nature. But here likewise two dangers threaten: A man may fail in his education to penetrate to the real roots of humanity and remain fixed in convention—a partial education of this sort is as bad as none—or he may suddenly collapse and neglect his self development. The well is there for all. No one is forbidden to take water from it. No matter how many come, all find what they need, for the well is dependable. It has a spring and never runs dry."[2]

Reading hexagram 48 was crucial to how we would structure our new school, The Well. The message confirmed for us the nature of the process of education. We committed to following the heart of the message as long as we ran The Well.

I was particularly struck by the last paragraph of the I Ching's description which dealt with the application to the individual of drawing water from the well. The reassurance that our education would be based on the infinite, divine nature of individual kids and not on a rigid curriculum directed us to focus our main attention on the students. Our studies would be built on the nature of the children and our perception of their needs. We would introduce a feast of academic and non-academic activities to determine which projects most enlivened the students. Everything made total sense.

The warning contained in that final paragraph further clarified our role. Our purpose was not to perpetuate what was conventional, but to deal with the depths of human nature. The depths! That meant some serious inquiry. Would these students be up for that? I decided to pursue the best literature I could find and to abandon all stories which were written as moral lessons for children or written for the sole purpose of teaching children how to read. For the next thirty-four years, the older children at The Well read and discussed many of the world's great spiritual stories, the masterful dramas of Sophocles, Aeschylus, Euripides, Shakespeare, Arthur Miller, Eugene O'Neill, Jean Girodeaux, and many others. We turned to Homer and the Greek myths which beautifully reveal, on many levels, the complex nature of mankind. I paid close attention to the thoughts and feelings of our students and inquired regularly about what was going on for them. Almost from the beginning, each student was given the power to call a Meeting at any point in the day to talk about whatever was important to him. The lives of kids merited this, because their experiences are, after all, as full and rich as that of adults, often more so.

The final warning of hexagram 48 was to look to self development, similar to what was called for in the famous inscription at Delphi, "Know thyself." So our discussions of literature with seventh- and eighth-graders focused on characters who struggled with self-knowledge. For the oldest kids, I included works like *Bhagavad Gita*, *Ramayana*, *Gilgamesh*, *Oedipus Rex*, *The Bacchae*, The Gospels of the New Testament, (especially the parables), and Plutarch's ancient biographies. We also read works by the historian Herodotus, as well as works by Homer, Plato, Lao Tzu, Huang Po, Geoffrey Chaucer, Leo Tolstoy, Herman Hesse, Henry Fielding, Henry David Thoreau, Ralph Waldo Emerson, Howard Pyle, Nathaniel Hawthorne, James Madison, John Adams, Thomas Jefferson, Mark Twain, Mary Renault, and C.S. Lewis. I included the poetry of Elizabeth Barrett Browning, Edna St. Vincent Millay, Emily Dickinson, William Blake, Kahil Gibran, Walt Whitman, and Robert Frost, etc.

I chose several main works of literature each year, according to the interests of each particular class, its reading ability, as well as what, at the time, interested me.

With most of the these books, students required a lot of background material and very close reading together at the beginning of a text. The first few pages often required several hours of reading and discussion. The next ten, several hours more. But there came a point when what had been read and discussed served as a strong basis of what would follow. In reading Plutarch's biographies of Greeks and Romans, each biography needed a lot of background information and a carefully measured start that allowed for hundreds of questions. But the process worked. The reading level of this literature was a little lower than what was commonly read in America at the end of the 18th Century—*The Bible* and *Pilgrim's Progress*, for example.

This idea of making self-knowledge a goal of education of the young is, indeed, radical. It is at odds with twentieth century education in America which is based, not on inner knowledge, but on the transfer of simplified knowledge, especially scientific knowledge about the outer world, to the individual mind as one might transfer data from a storage disc to a computer program. The standard applied is

Authority without wisdom is like a heavy ax without an edge, fitter to bruise than to polish.
Anne Bradstreet

accuracy. To give priority to the treasures which lie dormant within an individual and to focus on the nature of humanity itself, countermands the current system, because it focuses more on the development of the individual than on what the individual must know, according to the educational "experts," in order to increase the Gross National Product. Of course, it is impossible to know what individuals will need to know in a world with a fluid economy and social structure, a world in which the amount of information available to students doubles every year.

Education which promotes individual development promotes individual expression and individual freedom. It goes against the grain of conformity. Modern education shuns primary sources that contain challenging ideas, and, instead, it embraces a system that requires thousands of simple, incremental steps of rote learning before turning to original sources, probably not until the college level. The use of primary source material also flies in the face of corporate interests and the educational priorities of teacher's colleges, teacher's unions, and educational administrators. We will return to this later. The almost exclusive use of text books today, written for any reading level defines and dominates the curriculum.

1 Three years after naming the school "The Well," the name was reconfirmed for us. An elderly man who was unaware that we were running a school on the property knocked on our door, asked if we were the new owners, and asked to come in. He presented us with a model of a sweep well which was originally on our property but was covered over when a driveway had been built many years ago. It was a pole and bucket design. He made the beautiful miniature because he thought the new owners should be aware of its unique design

2 from hexagram 48 of The I Ching, Bollingen Series translated by Richard Wilhelm from Chinese into German, by Cary F. Baynes from German into English

Community and Inclusion

From the hexagram of The Well in the *I Ching* Toni and I took the image of water in the well as a symbol for the vital life force and as the symbol for intelligence. As people come together at a well to draw the water and to share it, according to the hexagram, so Well School people would come together to share life and knowledge. The water is for everyone; it is forbidden to no one; everyone is included. Did not the hexagram relate the drawing of water to education? Because of our experiences with Native Americans in Alaska, it all made sense.

It was as a teacher among the Eskimos that all the walls of separation that we had experienced in our earlier lives came down, disappeared. Thank God! Although these people had been brutally shamed and broken by their experience with the twin powers of church and school, institutions which consistently expounded on the inferiority of Eskimo language and culture, and though many of the native people were angry and a large number had escaped into alcoholism, they were, nevertheless, a people who shared whatever they had with each other.

Their community life was still based on openness and generosity. In Barrow, a group of men had killed a whale from an ice shelf in the Arctic Ocean where they had been camped for a week. For a day and a half, while the men cut and divided the huge creature they had raised onto the ice, members of the community came, with sleds or without, and took away portions of that catch. Like ants flocking to the sugar that sustained them, no one was denied a full portion.

I was shocked at their complete generosity. How could people so poor afford to be so generous? I was shocked that children were not constantly managed by their parents but were free to spend a night at the many houses in the community. Wherever they stayed, they would be well-fed, well taken care of, well-disciplined. Rather than one set of parents, each child had a hundred.

I was also shocked by the openness of the Eskimo people, who don't use their energy to project an image of how good or clever or superior they are. They do not use their ego to create separations or classes of society. Their simple vulnerability and their lack of critical judgment made me question my own assumptions about the necessity of always protecting and defending oneself.

My negative experience as a student and my positive experience as a teacher recommended and illumined the choice of Inclusion (hereafter used to designate the principle of uniting people) as the foundation of our new school. The Well would not be just a school; it would be a community. That would be a challenge for me, for I was better suited to be a loner than a community member.

I tried to understand the essence of Inclusion so that I might apply this principle in Peterborough, quite a different culture from the Inuit. Inclusion, as I understood it, is itself a paradigm, simple in purpose, complex in nature. Inclusion implies a full constellation of simple ideas and purposeful attitudes. They are reflected in several definable aspects without which Inclusion would cease to exit. The stars in this constellation include:

> A devotion to truth
> A sense of belonging
> Honesty kindly expressed
> Openness to change and discovery
> Respect for all
> Honoring others
> Fulfilling individual responsibility
> Brotherhood and sisterhood
> Teamwork
> Spontaneous helpfulness
> Forgiving human weakness, human mistakes

These are the same qualities that a well-functioning family might display.

Inclusion always expresses generosity. "Would you like to play with us," comes from an extension of self. If you are new to a community and a member of that community says, "Hi, I'm Jack. Come join us, we're playing capture the flag. You can be on my team," there is no doubt about whether you are accepted, or honored, or safe, because you are experiencing the full constellation of inclusion. Inclusion shatters the us/them dichotomy and creates one family. New, exciting possibilities based on trust and love rush in to fill the void of exclusivity. Where there is only one family, we are home, safe, and free.

For me, what is noticeably absent from the paradigm of Inclusion is the employment of shame and guilt to manipulate others; what is missing is cruel humor, cynicism, and intimidation; what is missing is the willful, separation of self from others and self from self. What is missing is the exhausting competition over who is in and who is out.

A safe environment extends the family for those who have found safety within their own families. It provides a whole new set of brothers and sisters. But for those who come from a family that practices ridicule and abuse, a safe environment provides a previously unknown refuge, a haven where self-expression and self-knowledge can flourish.

Natural affection within families is often expressed by physical contact, by hugging, a hand on the shoulder, a stroke to the hair. That touch, as many know, is soothing, reassuring, and healing.

The Well not only allowed contact between kids or between kids and teachers, but it strongly encouraged and reinforced it. Distance suggests disapproval. When we are upset with someone, it is natural to avoid contact. And they in turn, sensing we are angry, move towards isolation and estrangement. This expression of separation needs no explaining; it is built into our body and our psyche. So does the meaning of body contact.

When someone is on edge and unsure of themselves, easy and natural contact implies joining together and reestablishes a sense of

Praise is well, compliment is well, but affection – that is the last and final and most precious reward that any man can win.
Mark Twain

confidence. If someone is ridiculed, hurt, or just freaking out, a hug can restore his sanity and tell him immediately he is OK. A teacher who senses that a student is intimidated by a math problem, can, with a little body contact, relax the child and talk them through their insecurity, letting them know that they are loved, whether they solve the problem or not.

Haven't we all read to a child while he or she lies snuggled into our lap? The contact both enriches and enlivens the activity. It prepares a secure and intimate place for a rich experience of reading.

Schools that prohibit contact automatically mandate an environment of isolation. To me, rules forbidding contact are nothing less than strong evidence of child abuse, because they deny the contact that one needs to feel safe and grounded and to fully function.

The homophobia of our larger society has a devastating effect on kids, particularly for children from age ten up. It creates a fear of touching that is unmatched since early Puritan times. Even accidental contact becomes subject to ridicule, and a single negative comment can

The Children's Hour

Between the dark and the daylight,
  When the night is beginning to lower,
Comes a pause in the day's occupations
  That is known as the Children's Hour.

I hear in the chamber above me
  The patter of little feet,
The sound of the door that is opened,
  And the voices soft and sweet.

From my study I see in the lamplight,
  Descending the broad hall stair,
Grave Alice, and laughing Allegra,
  And Edith with golden hair.

A whisper and then a silence:
  Yet I know by their merry eyes
They are plotting and planning together
  To take me by surprise.

A sudden rush from the stairway,
  A sudden raid from the hall!
By three doors left unguarded
  They enter my castle wall!

They climb up into my turret
  O'er the arms and back of my chair;
If I try to escape, they surround me,
  They seem to be everywhere.

They almost devour me with kisses,
  Their arms about me entwine,
Till I think of the Bishop of Bingen
  In his Mouse-Tower on the Rhine!

Do you think, O blue-eyed banditti,
  Because you have scaled the wall,
Such an old moustache as I am
  Is not a match for you all!

I have you fast in my fortress,
  And will not let you depart,
But put you down into the dungeon
  In the round-tower of my heart.

And there I will keep you forever,
  Yes, forever and a day,
Till the walls shall crumble to ruin,
  and moulder the dust away!

Henry Wadsworth Longfellow

freeze the life force. The taboo on contact, with its endless innuendos, sensitizes and paralyzes relationships among the young and redefines a healthy friendship as something sexually disgusting. Any behavior which creates excessive consciousness of sexuality propels one toward the kind of obsessive thought that is characteristic of people with a sexual addiction. Listen to casual conversation between kids; sexuality is usually the first line of attack, especially among boys. "You homo!" "You fag!" "You queer!" enters habitual vocabulary even before age ten.

Ridicule has become a cultural pastime, and many boys avoid entire fields of endeavor that used to belong to men—music, dance, art, theater and even academics—because the pain of a single negative comment can destroy one's sense of safety.

Our greatest fear is abandonment and the vulnerability it exposes. The very threat of becoming socially excluded corrupts honesty. If this sword of Damocles stops self-expression, one loses one's wholeness, one's integrity, and one's connection to sensitivity, beauty, and truth. Fear of ridicule and fear of intimacy are not just additional issues in the long list of school issues. They are *the* issues for most school-age children. They determine one's ability to express oneself in a thousand ways. They determine whether or not one dares to be aboveboard, guileless, genuine, real. If we cannot speak our own truth, what then is left of our dignity.

When self-expression and honesty are forfeited, we live in the prison of our mind where self-knowledge is out of reach and spirit becomes inaccessible. The success of those that flourish through intimidation and fear—whether they be bullies, mean-spirited vultures, bigots, those without scruples, the in-crowd, the Mafia, or fascists—ultimately depends on fearful individuals who cannot speak their minds.

Many use reports of child abuse and kidnapping as a rationale to train their children into fear of closeness with anybody except blood relationships. Yet, the great majority of cases of child abuse and kid-

> *For I kept my heart from assenting to anything fearing to fall headlong; but by hanging in suspense I was the worst killed.*
> **St. Augustine**

napping are done by blood relatives. Instructions to avoid closeness teach a lack of faith in mankind that may never be undone. If the intention is to prepare kids to live in a hostile and alien world, it certainly does that. But the emotional cost is brutal and irreparable.

So the conscious purpose of The Well was just the opposite: to promote Community and Inclusion and to release children from fear-based thoughts which suggest that every stranger is a potential predator. If children are to reveal their brilliance, humanity, and divinity, they must trust, and trust deeply, not just their relatives, but their community as a whole. We all require a safe place if we are ever to break the cycle of fear. Children accustomed to experiencing contact in a friendly, casual way do not make the paranoid presumption that all touching is sexual.

How do we encourage contact between kids? By encouraging hugs to express heartfelt gratitude or forgiveness. By including physical activities like circle games, massage, soccer, and other contact sports. And most importantly, by approving of such appropriate, natural expressions of affection. Teachers and parents who hug each other and are available for hugs from students serve as role models for healthy contact. They bind a community together with active expressions of love and Inclusion.

A neurotic person may have a feeling of terror when he approaches the realization that some genuine fondness is being offered to him.

Karen Horney

Meeting

The Well opened its doors in September of 1967 to sixteen students, seven of them Garland cousins. It grew until it numbered about one hundred day students, although throughout the years, Toni and I accepted a few boarders. Class size ranged from two to sixteen; the average was ten, a considerable advantage for teachers who wished to be in close contact with their students. At the beginning, Toni taught grades one through three, and I taught grades four through eight.

The Well's best mechanism for supporting Inclusion was regular meetings devoted to open discussion. One fall day during the first year of The Well, I sensed some negativity among members of the class and asked everyone to put their books and papers away, move tables and desks out of a central area, and sit in a circle. We held hands for about a minute to establish the sense of the circle, the sense of unity. Then we had, what was for me, a wonderful, open talk, and the negativity disappeared for the rest of the day. The next morning, one of my students was removed from the school, without any discussion, because the parents feared we were practicing some kind of voodoo.

Nevertheless, Meeting (Meeting will be capitalized in the text when it refers to convening for the express purpose of raising consciousness) became a regular class at The Well. When the school expanded and we had more classrooms, one Meeting was established for the lower grades and one for the upper grades. Often a single class would have their own Meeting. Once a week the whole school met together.

Meeting served to air disputes, express hurt feelings, and remedy exclusive behavior. It provided an open-ended time period to allow hidden feelings to surface. It provided a structured place for kids to air their complaints with each other, to talk about friendships, and to discuss elements of their home life. (We let parents know that if they would believe only half of what they heard about us, we would believe only half of what their kids told us about them.)

Meetings also gave kids a chance to air their grievances about teachers, and it offered teachers an opportunity to confront their students in an open forum where all could learn. Of course, many problems were settled out of Meeting, one-on-one, but when that failed, there was always Meeting where anything could be discussed. When trust had been broken (somebody had stolen something, cheated, or lied), Meeting served as a familiar environment in which to plan better ways of reacting to awkward or painful situations. Sally could tell Susie that she was really mad at her for going off to be alone with Joan, and Susie had to listen to Sally and respond, because the community was there to witness the discussion. The entire group could then discuss alternative behaviors which would hurt no one.

The rules of etiquette for Meeting included:

1. Speak from your heart, not from your mind. Look at the person you're talking to.

2. Allow somebody to finish what they need to say.

3. Look at, listen to, and respond individually to every person that talks to you.

> Namaste! I honor the place in you in which the entire universe dwells. I honor the love, the truth, the light and the peace in you. When you are in that place in you and I am in that place in me, we are one...Namaste!

4. Even if you're angry, you must show respect with your choice of words and you're tone of voice.

5. If you have done something similar to what a person being reprimanded did, admit to it before you say anything else.

> Thousands of candles can be lighted from a single candle, and the life of he candle will not be shortened. Happiness never decreases by being shared.
>
> **Buddha**

6. Don't repeat what someone has just said.

> *In spite of the pain that our friend's faults cause us we keep up a fantastic pretense of blindness in order that we may remain tolerable to each other. That is why we have to talk behind people's back. There is no other chance of talking freely.*
> **Robert Lynd**

7. Show compassion for the mistakes of others.

Although Meeting was in many ways a protective environment, it also supported telling the truth. I trace Meeting's origin to the plains Indians of America who formed a circle of rocks to represent the many ways of seeing which were linked to the four directions of a compass. It was recognized that each person in the circle had a different perspective of the subject under discussion. The vision of the group, as a whole, represented the truth that was sought; each individual's opinion was a limited perspective. Our circle was also an occasion for telling one's truth when a situation seemed out of balance. One or more members of a circle might criticize someone for cheating or for being pretentious, hypocritical, or phony. These were among the dominant issues for kids. They were most interested in sorting out reality from fantasy, for they yearned for an identity which was based on truth.

One may be exposed by someone as a trouble-maker. Dealing with an unacknowledged truth about oneself, is unsettling at best. Fearing exposure, as anyone raiding the cookie jar without permission knows, is uncomfortable. Feeling exposed is both painful and humiliating. We feel our power drain away and unconsciously call on our "shadow self" to defend us, to justify our actions.

The group needed to be educated about the universality of man's shadow, the tendency for all of us to unconsciously hide and deny what we are ashamed of in order to project an enhanced image. They needed to understand that the shadow is only a part of the total self, that one may only grow by courageously confronting it and moving on.

The need to appear good and to be perceived as perfect retards growth and causes much unnecessary suffering. Parents praise their children for being good and scold them for being bad; they create the need for children to pretend to be what they are not in order to receive approval and avoid rejection. This need has created generations of hypocrites in our society. The greatest deterrent to learning, in my experience, is the fear of being wrong; fear, in fact, stops the flow of natural intelligence and causes people to act and feel stupid.

The myth that there are good and bad people is divisive and undermines our true self. Nobody is good; nobody is bad. The attempt to be good or to appear good creates a great wedge between our true inner being and our mask; the habit of doing so separates us from our own self.

I find the conversation recorded in the New Testament book of Matthew 19:16-30 illuminating. Jesus's response to a man who calls him "Good Master" was "Why callest thou me good? There is none good but one, that is, God." The man proclaims his goodness; he claims to have followed all the commandments throughout his life. Jesus replies, "If thou wilt be perfect, go and sell that thou hast, and give to the poor, and thou shalt have treasure in heaven: and come and follow me." When the man departs in sorrow, Jesus tells his disciples, "Verily I say unto you, That a rich man shall hardly enter the kingdom of heaven. And again I say unto you, It is easier for a camel to go through the eye of a needle, than for a rich man to enter into the kingdom of God."

The story speaks to me in a symbolic as well as a literal way. A large part of this man's "riches" was his inflated self-image of being good and his perfect record of never having broken a single commandment. He is unable to move out of his "goodness" and into his *innate* perfection, because he is a prisoner of a concept that being good equates to being superior. Good people are unable to hear truth, to awaken. Their own "goodness" prevents them.

Our shadow self, which some may call bad, is potentially a source of great humility and understanding. All growth depends on acknowledging the fly in our ointment. Growth occurs whenever our own discomfort moves us in a new direction. We become larger and more compassionate whenever we adopt, instead of repudiate, our own shadow. Our dark side, if embraced, lends us its powerful energy which can now be used in productive ways. It often leads us to exciting careers, helping others to recognize and accept their own shadow.

Harriet was a "good" girl; she strove to be recognized by adults not only for her academic achievements, but for her generosity or acts of charity. Her peers implicitly mistrusted her. When acts of mischief occurred sometime between the end of classes and when students were picked up by their parents, the feelings of trust between teachers and students and among students began to erode. The contents of tubes of paint were found squeezed out on objects in a classroom. The hands of clocks were bent at awkward angles, items from bagged lunches disappeared, as did pens and pencils from personal cubbies. Harriet was "nailed" in class meeting by her infuriated peers who had witnessed a few of her antics. Kids complained that they were not being trusted because of her vandalism and stealing. Many voiced their anger. But Harriet coolly protested that she was being unfairly accused, that she was innocent of all wrongdoing, and that everyone would find out the real truth about her in time. A parent who was attending this meeting was shocked at the abuse poured on this child. How could people so mistreat a defenseless child. Why didn't the teachers put an end to the unproved accusations.

At the Meeting a week later, Harriet still maintained her complete innocence, even though many had witnessed her continued stealing. The same parent who had previously questioned Harriet's treatment now wanted Harriet removed from the school for being a threat to the other students' possessions, including those of her own children.

Harriet's bad behavior stopped soon after, but she did not admit to her vandalism or stealing for a long time to come. She was not kicked out of school. When her parents were notified of her shadow activities, they were very accepting, even thankful for the information, well aware of her ability to be devious. They were grateful for our patience and acknowledged many transformations that were happening for her at home. Harriet proved not only to be a fine academic, but also a fine actress, singer, and a compassionate human being. Her genuineness of heart and spirit deepened. After she graduated, she returned to The Well as a volunteer to teach projects during Project Month.

Alice lied and cheated excessively and dramatically covered up each deceit with a new con job, a new story to either excuse her behavior or to elicit sympathy for herself. On having her fabrications revealed, her shame and remorse, displayed as weeping and flailing, were bottomless. She convinced her peers of her incurable liver disease, making them promise not to reveal her tragic secret. She became the center of attention, eliciting constant sympathy and consternation from others. She also became an outstanding performer, musically and dramatically, where her ability to dissemble and assume roles worked to her advantage. She was involved in a secret life outside of school which involved alcohol, drugs, and sex, while still a seventh- or eighth-grader.

But she also transformed herself in those same years. As a young teenager she became an open, amazing, perceptive, creative person, an excellent student, and a seeker of beauty and truth. After she graduated from The Well, she excelled in boarding school, where she counseled peers to avoid drugs and to face their shadow side. In college, she dared to pursue excellence. She also arranged to study abroad and experienced life in England, India, and several African countries. She had a towering free spirit, high standards, well defined moral limits, and an abiding love of life.

She has great power today because she experienced great discomfort at a young age while she consciously attempted to confront and integrate her shadow into her ego. Her wish to be the center of attention, which brought her untold embarrassment when she was a young student, was legitimately realized as a young adult. She learned to develop and maximize her talents and to use them appropriately. Her sense of adventure was and *is* awesome. Today she is one of the most honest and open people I know, one who can laugh joyfully at her follies.

For me, it is where shadow meets the light that miracles occur. Children who learn that their shadow may be expressed and brought into the open without forfeiting the love of others, exchange, in a relatively short time, their fears and deception for genuine self-expression and raw honesty; they learn to follow their own heart and to experience their own greatness.

As a fifth grader, Maria, told and read stories of the Buddha in class meeting because she wanted to share her love of Buddha. She was very much an innocent child of nature and that was reflected in her natural beauty. In conferences, we learned of her dark side from her mother. Maria could be cruel and cold and uncompromising. Could that be true? But when Maria turned to cheating in math, over a period of time, the subsequent revelation in Meeting clearly tortured her. We waited for a confession because all the evidence pointed to her duplicity. Answer books occasionally have mistakes, as you may know, but when a child duplicates the mistakes as well as the correct answers, something is up! This star student, who so idolized the Buddha, this paragon of virtue, had to recognize her human failings. Eventually, with tears, then sobs, she expressed her shame and guilt. Perhaps she was not prepared for the love that followed, but she seemed more overcome by the forgiveness of others than by the betrayal of herself. As she immediately deepened as a person and grew in beauty within, one could see the inspiration on her face. Only in owning our shadow is its power to transform the heart released. It is only through loving an imperfect self that we can afford to be compassionate toward the shadows of others.

For all the kids who seemed to grow tremendously in the years at The Well, there were also those to whom we could not give enough love. They left us still feeling they were not good enough.

Holes in the walls indicated that Johnny's home was regularly

> **The Tide**
> The tide pulls me out to sea
> Where I have never swum
> And sets me on a sand bar
> Where all the fishes come.
>
> The fears that chain me to my past
> Declare their presence still,
> But as I gambol on the shore
> New pleasures I fulfill.
> **Jay Garland**

trashed by an abusive, alcoholic father. He and his younger brother often slept in the barn to avoid horrible confrontations. Johnny had a permanent look of sadness in his eyes, and a load of guilt lived in his sunken shoulders. "Why are you so sad today, Johnny?" asked Toni on the school climb up a nearby mountain. "Because," Johnny replied, with a rope of snot hanging from his nose, "I lost my friend yesterday. He was just walking around our neighborhood and he fell in an open septic tank and drowned." Johnny was undone, and no amount of sympathy penetrated his mood, although, as his mother told us the next day, "Johnny just made up the story. He lies all the time." Johnny's fantasies contained a lot of truth for him, because they expressed indirectly, what he could not express directly—his great sorrow about the cruelties he participated in and witnessed.

Despite many efforts by all the teachers and all his friends in Meeting, Johnny was unable to accept his greatness. He finally refused to come back to The Well, and we lost him. We felt we had failed him.

Sandi, who had been adopted at age two, by a mother who already had two kids at The Well, was very smart and alternately friendly and hostile. In eighth grade she occasionally talked in class about her secret, hidden life of badness with a half-smile on her lips and terror in her eyes. It prompted a few other students to reveal hidden aspects of their lives, but Sandi always declined to be explicit herself.

For years, seventh- and eighth-graders had an American History class, which included a simulation of an 18th century village set in Virginia. Kids studied various occupations, gave reports, and then role-played at those jobs. They also kept a journal of an entire fictional family, writing each day about something that had happened to one of their family members from that person's point of view. They bought and sold property, and, by throwing dice and consulting charts, random things happened to their fictional characters. The class banker's record indicated that Sandi's fictional family (the mother of that family was a midwife) was falling ever more deeply into debt. Sandi contracted with another family to sell one of her children to them, a novel strategy, in order to raise some money to pay her debts. To Sandi, it seemed a simple and clever thing to do at the time. Anne-Marie, a teacher who was aware of Sandi's own adoption confronted Sandi and asked, "How could you give away your own child? Isn't that a heartless thing to do?" Sandi got her message and was heartbroken to have done to her "child" what had been done to her. Later, she brightened considerably.

Our dark side internalizes whatever injustice we perceive we have suffered and then plays out that injustice with others, unconsciously, of course, until we acknowledge the full dimensions of who we are. At Meeting, in Conference, and in class, Sandi worked on the issue of being disposable trash and played it out in her life. Although one of our teachers took her to Mexico to meet and reconcile with her birth mother, total forgiveness may still remain a future challenge for Sandi.

Before Jack entered The Well in sixth grade, he had twice attempted suicide. He loved his teacher immediately and made steady progress. He had great days at school and, as reported by his mother, horrible days at home. He loved to be at school and was greatly appreciated by his classmates. Yet, for a year he resisted leaving his home to come to school each morning. He needed to regain a positive relationship with his parents who had expressed their disappointment at his not living up to his potential. He was a kind and brilliant child whose great wit attested to his clear perception of hypocrisy and paradox. When Jack graduated, he was a favorite of everyone at school, but he still struggled from time to time with bouts of depression.

After leaving The Well, Jack attempted suicide again in high school; he was obviously still haunted by his own demons. He interrupted his college years to return to The Well to become my assistant for two years. He was an amazing teacher and a great friend to students. He contributed great joy and optimism to our community. Years later, he visited us and revealed that he had tried to take his life again. His life continued to alternate between times of feeling great about himself and bouts of despair which totally overcame him.

All children try, in their individual way, to integrate and reconcile the conflicting aspects of light and darkness within their personalilty. Do educators have a role to play in helping people see that the "good" and the "bad" can live together. I think so, because as long as man remains permanently divided, he is capable of endless atrocities and continued cruelty to himself and others. Do individuals need to face their own pettiness, their own hatreds, their own fears? It is a blessing, in fact, to do so, and it is a main component of authentic education. For only then can education encourage growth, development, and transformation. Only the isolated self believes, in its own embrace of ignorance, that it is fooling others when it attempts to hide its shadow.

Most children abhor hypocrisy. Educators who refuse to deal with hypocrisy in their environment only exaggerate the pretense. It is necessary to have teachers who examine their own hypocrisy and who serve as an example of honesty by admitting their foibles. It releases them and their students from playing frustrating games. Discomfort and anxiety are a sign of hypocrisy, signals which call for change. If we cannot sleep at night, our anxiety notifies us that something is amiss, out-of-balance, overlooked. To heed the call moves us out of anxiety and into action. If one's heart pounds, a response is needed, if only to speak one's truth. If we swallow our own dis-ease we remain small; if we respond, we expand our own life. The inner depth of our being always alerts us to crucial, unfulfilled needs. If we refuse to listen , we are compelled to deaden our senses with addictive substances or with addictive behavior in order to silence the relentless inner voice. All the drug and alcohol abuse legislation in the world does not address the causes of addiction: loss of contact with inner self and lack of integration of self. Workaholics must remain busy lest they hear the voice within. Those who live in hell, or create a hell for others, ignore the guidance of their true being, because they have been convinced to look outside themselves for the causes of their dis-ease.

So, in Meeting, we allowed anyone who was put on the spot by his teachers or his peers for being irresponsible or dishonest to experience the discomfort and then respond. We allowed the teacher, as well, to experience the discomfort caused by children who needed to voice what they saw as clear injustice or hypocrisy on the teacher's part, so all could move from repressive silence to a living response. These healing encounters, within a supportive "family" were part of our regular, rich life together. Any parent who heard that their child was subject to group pressure was invited to attend any or all Meetings to decide whether our process was abusive or loving. No parent who attended Meeting ever removed their child from The Well.

On the other hand, there were parents who did not accept the invitation to come to Meeting. They expressed their clear discomfort with their children discussing, in our forum, their family secrets. Although the power of the secret to exclude, torture, and repress is legendary, keeping secrets will always have it advocates. Our purpose in sponsoring an open meeting was simply to give a voice to all. Since we thought that keeping a secret introduced emotional poison into one's own being, we recommended that when asked, "Can you keep a secret?", a healthy and honest response is "No!"

Occasionally, opposition to meetings came from teachers who wanted to avoid the scrutiny of their students in order to better preserve their own authority. So Meeting, in our eyes, also stripped teachers of any excessive authority that they might exercise in an isolated classroom. The democratic structure of our meeting expressed our strong stance on the equality of all beings.

The very existence of Meeting also allowed us to have an open campus where older children could play in their free time without adult supervision. We believed the dignity of man requires unstructured, unsupervised time. On the fifty-plus acres of the school property, there were open areas, fields, and woodland. There were opportunities for kids to stay out of the view of adults while on their own. We knew much of what happened out of our sight, because three of the

---

Real Riches

Tis little I could care for pearls
Who own the ample sea;
Or brooches, when the Emperor

With rubies pelteth me;
Or gold, who am the Prince of Mines;
Or diamonds, when I see
A diadem to fit a dome
Continual crowning me.

Emily Dickinson

kids were our own children, and they loved to recite, at dinner time, the details of their play.

The most exciting activity for them was building, either building tree houses or miniature homes and palaces. The slate that had been left over from building a roof more than fifty years earlier served as a means of monetary exchange for the children. And sometimes a group would build a fort or form a club and exclude other students. Such exclusions were often aired and remedied in Meeting.

To meet at all, we must open one's eyes to another; and there is no true conversation, no matter how many words are spoken, unless the eye, unveiled and listening, opens itself to the other.
Jessamyn West

Meeting was key for the school to function harmoniously. When Meeting failed to work, as it did from time to time, students would secretly pay for what they said in Meeting after the Meeting was over. Everything else suffered. At times a group of very aggressive students caused a "coup," and so intimidated others behind the scenes so that the truth remained unspoken. Then Meeting would devolve into a phony sweetness and have as its main content announcements, scheduling questions, or trite conversation.

Meeting at its best allowed all feelings and opinions. It repaired broken trust. It created an atmosphere of unity. But much of Meeting also allowed kids to say what they admired about each other and to express their joy and gratitude in being together. It fostered storytelling, guided meditation, discussion of ideas, spontaneous role-playing, the presentation of skits or projects, discussion of current events, massages, and singing together.

True goodness lies not in the negation of badness, but in the mastery of it. It is the miracle that turns the tumult of chaos into the dance of beauty. True education is that power of miracle, that ideal of creation.
Rabindranath Tagore

Open and honest Meeting discussions created an environment in which there was little covert cruelty. The sense of safety and trust changed everything. Our students flourished academically, exceeding all expectations; their art and music were breathtaking, they took care of each other, and they celebrated each others' accomplishments. Every day, hundreds of personal compliments were shared informally in classes. For all to excel became the norm, the standard. "Great job," "I wish I could do that," "That is so awesome," "I love what you did," and "Cool," were responses from kid to kid concerning presentations,

Every individual who is not creative has a negative, narrow, exclusive taste and succeeds in depriving creative being of his energy and life.
Johann Wolfgang von Goethe

tests, projects, or other acomplishments. Everyone was a winner and felt like one. When everyone in a class or in a school soars, it is only because negative comments, sarcasm, ugly facial gestures, and evil eye expressions (whether on the part of students or teachers) disappear.

One regular feature of Meeting was the option to go into the center of the circle to hear what everyone else thought about you. Part of the tradition was first to be asked whether you just wanted to hear the good news or whether you also welcomed negative criticism. Never, in all our years, did a student opt just to hear the positive observations. In fact, the main motivation for a student or a teacher to ask to go into the center was to learn how people really saw him or her and to get feedback from thirty to fifty people. Some years, nobody would put themselves on the hot spot until January or February. But once the ice was broken, others yearned to discover how peers and teachers saw them.

The process occasioned by just one individual in the center took from twenty minutes to an hour, depending on how well you were known to the whole group and whether you asked for clarifications of the comments of your peers. Individuals around the circle might simply say, "You annoy me," or "I admire you." But more often, they would expand their comments and mention the specific qualities they saw in the person, or they would ask the person to change a certain behavior, or they would request to spend more time with a child.

Usually, the compliments far outweighed the criticisms. But a child who saw little good in others and who was also annoying to many, nevertheless, received about 50 percent very positive feedback. Often, just being open to criticism altered the perception of others and allowed them to notice the positive as well as the negative. In either case, the result of the shower of comments made the one who was under scrutiny feel more valued and more wanted than they had previously thought possible.

I usually made myself vulnerable and went to the center of the circle when I noticed that my students were not taking care of my needs in class, and I wondered what hostility or indifference lay behind their ignoring me. Mostly, I received reassurances, but the criticisms were always more helpful, because they inevitably broke the ice and suggested ways for me to meet their needs.

Even in a safe atmosphere, many children needed help finding the appropriate words to express themselves. Many were emotionally illiterate; they were unable to read their own feelings. Their early training had made certain feelings like anger and jealousy unacceptable and, therefore, unavailable to consciousness. They needed help building a vocabulary of feelings, a list of words to identify simple emotional states. They benefitted from simple role playing or participation in dramatic performances in order to work through their need to express the inexpressible.

Since emotions supply the energy for changing habits, for honoring and fulfilling our choices, it is critical to be fluent in the language of feelings, to have one's emotional life at one's command. To know oneself, one must practice identifying the grand sweep and variety of emotions which pass through one's being on a daily basis.

For Adults? Life Institute?

Our experience with Life Institute both confirmed and expanded our understanding of Meeting. For me, it provided an opportunity to look at myself separate from the setting of The Well and to thoroughly explore my relationship with Toni. Although Life Institute was limited to adults, the parallels between the two forums were enlightening.

In 1977, when Meeting had been practiced for about ten years, my belief in the power of a circle of people trying to improve their understanding of themselves was re-affirmed. Toni and I were visited by friends who urged us to attend Life Institute, a five-day workshop that was given in several locations in the country, including our town of Peterborough and the city of Boston. They asked us to trust them, that they had found it invaluable for themselves, and that the workshop was impossible to explain. That rang a bell!

Although Life Institute had no formal connection with The Well, I experienced Life Institute as an adult extension of our school Meeting. The combination of direct honesty within an emotionally-safe environment was common to both. And, submitting myself to the scrutiny of strangers made me more aware of the dynamics of Meeting and its importance to The Well.

Our experience at Life Institute in Boston shook up our marriage. Toni and I had a long talk on the way home about whether we would stay together. In the end, we re-committed to a relationship with higher standards of integrity, honesty, and love. Our higher level of energy affected the school in a positive way.

In this country that emphasizes education and degrees and that has a multitude of colleges and universities that teach both mainstream and arcane courses, most well-educated parents, including the author, have no training in either the role of a marriage partner or in the role of a parent. Yet, these are two of the most difficult jobs any individual will ever have. Parents, therefore, often welcome an educational experience for themselves which clarifies and enlightens the experience of marriage and/or parenting.

Most marriages contain areas of conflict and ugly patterns of behavior which are hard to resolve or change. Ignoring those signs of discord and disunity only leads to an emotional separation that robs both partners of their integrity. Repetitive fights do nothing to bridge the gap or heal the separation. I am familiar with these patterns in my own marriage, as well as in those of my friends and acquaintances.

Having children usually resolves nothing that was unresolved before, for the children merely tend to become silent witnesses to the power struggle of the adults. Often, if there are two or more children in the family, each parent "adopts" his or her own special child. But such special pairings only more deeply divide the family and postpone the resolution of issues.

The dynamics of special relationships, whether between two adults or two adults with one or more children, often revolve around efforts to control another through guilt, fear, or shame. Sometimes one parent has the upper hand in terms of power; sometimes the child holds the balance of power. The love/hate cycle of special relationships is as old as history, because few have learned to disengage and to totally forgive what lies in their past. Unresolved resentment in a marriage is unconsciously maintained on a daily basis and depletes the energy available for the present. This leaves little energy or will power to commit to resolving current issues. And the shame attached to seeking a therapist or mediator usually precludes getting help to seek a resolution.

One cannot solve systemic problems with one's old consciousness. Maintaining the old level of consciousness contributes to not facing

To ask that one's own high self should forgive one's own trespasses is the hardest prayer to answer that we can ever offer up ... We cannot forgive others in any comprehensive sense unless we have first learnt to forgive ourselves.

Henry Havelock Ellis

issues and to not being totally honest. In welcoming more awareness and in seeking help from higher powers or from a source of wisdom greater than one's own, one releases old addictive attitudes and viewpoints and is able to move to a new level of thinking, feeling, and doing. (After my experience at Life Institute, I visited my good friend, Tony, who, on first seeing me, said, "What's happened to you? I see someone different.")

There is a myth that says if one member of a couple grows spiritually, it will create strife within the marriage. Indeed, there is ample strife and conflict in relationships even when no one changes. Couples rarely raise their consciousness simultaneously, and it seems ridiculous to delay becoming more conscious while waiting for one's partner to see what you see. No, the new perspectives are meant to be shared. If that challenges the other, it's all to the good. Separation and divorce do not end life; sometimes they allow life to flower. Life itself is a school where we are meant to grow up, to enlarge our vision, to forgive, to move on, and to claim our divine inheritance.

Each time a parent grows, kids are released from a burden. They are free to more consciously examine their own life, to more respectfully follow their deepest instincts, interests, and needs. When a parent exemplifies the purpose of life and moves from a more limited tribal and group thought process, to a more tolerant and more compassionate viewpoint, new possibilities occur for the child, as well. Even a stranger who brings an enlarged perspective, influences and moves us. Imagine how much more influential it is when a parent lets us see new possibilities and new perspectives.

Family Conferences

Twice a year at The Well, usually packed into a long weekend, we held Family Conferences which included two to six teachers, (never one!) the parents, and, in the case of a student in fifth grade or above, the student himself. At these meetings, we discussed the academic, artistic, and social progress, as well as the personal growth of each student. We also addressed any issues parents had with teachers or teachers with parents or students. Conferences connected the parents not just with the viewpoint of the classroom teachers but also with the insights of teacher's assistants and specialty teachers, including instructors of foreign language, and art. Bringing all these people together in one place created both a clarity and a perspective which allowed us all to make more informed and more effective decisions.

It also provided a forum for parents, teachers, and students to speak their mind. In the early years, some of these conferences turned into marathon sessions, lasting for more than two to three hours, especially if there were two or three siblings involved. They were great opportunities for direct communication, so Toni and I tended to be very honest whether we were given permission by the parents to do so or not. Often, in the interests of helping the child, we had specific suggestions for the parents, which were either appreciated or resented. Sometimes, there was a huge breakthrough when a child was supported for being totally honest about old hidden issues or feelings. In general, we noted that each round of conferences produced results that were, on the whole, positive and helpful; there were always a few that seemed unproductive or negative. In any case, over the course of a weekend, our conversations with students and their families provided a tremendous amount of useful information that helped us do a better job as teachers.

So much good resulted from our meetings with families because we had an opportunity to create a bridge between home and school life, and all of us were conscious of what we were working towards. Often when a child was asked what she thought her parents expected of her in school, her response revealed a great disparity between what she thought and what her parents wanted. Toni and I were both shocked at our own children's versions of our expectations for them. (At the conferences which involved our own children, other Well staff—usually Libby, Katy or Carol—assumed control.) So much is assumed by children when messages are not clearly articulated. Some children, although they receive praise for many accomplishments, assume that parents only care about grades, teacher evaluations, and achievement tests. Children assume that it is a required part of a parent's job to flatter them or give them a boost when their confidence is low. As a result, they automatically discount whatever expression of admiration or adulation comes their way from a parent. Other children assume that their parents want them to be obedient and passive and to stay out of trouble, when the parents, in fact, yearn to hear their child's perspective on many things and want to connect to their son's or daughter's curiosity and sense of beauty.

Many parents settle for crumbs from their children; they are so grateful to receive just a token that they rarely give the child the responsibilities which would create a healthy sense of self-pride. In a conference, when a a seven-year-old describes his potential contributions to his family, I often respond by listing for the child, in the presence of his family, some things that seven-year-olds are fully capable of doing, and doing well and cheerfully. For example: setting the breakfast table, making breakfast for the family or cleaning up after the meal; making their own lunch; making their bed and cleaning their room; asking what else they can do to help out before leaving for school; wishing their parents a great day; thanking parents for the ride to school; telling their parents at night what they found beautiful, exciting, and interesting during the school day; inquiring about what kind of day a parent had; attending to homework after a snack at home without being reminded; doing whatever regular jobs they are responsible for; doing the laundry; setting up for dinner or washing dishes afterwards; giving thanks; doing something special for siblings or parents; or volunteering to go to bed at an agreed on time. This used to be the standard when Americans lived on farms or ranches and when children were needed to regularly contribute their share so that a self-respecting family could survive.

Most parents are floored, symbolically of course. Most children are intrigued at the possibility of being needed and are also a little fearful of their trustworthiness to deliver on a regular basis. Many families ignored our suggestions of age-appropriate responsibilities, but many immediately put into practice what they saw was both healthy and possible. They decided they didn't want a "show dog," they wanted a "working dog" who took pride in his ability to cheerfully help sustain the family. Most families need all the help they can get, all the good will, all the consciousness of how to work together as a team in order to live in an upbeat, optimistic fashion. When children are expected to help shoulder the load of modern family life, they flourish, their self-esteem soars, their attitude brightens. When I ask children in conference whether they would be willing to up the ante, most answer "yes" without hesitation.

Many parents, especially working parents, indulge their children out of guilt. Because they have not provided constant support for their offspring, they feel they are deficient as parents and owe their children everything they can think to buy for them. These parents fail to realize how incredible and loving they are in dealing with all that is expected of them. In a balanced family, all members contribute so that everyone has time of their own to do just what they especially love.

Many families noticed that what worked in our conferences might work just as well at home. They scheduled their own family conferences each weekend to assess the give and take of the past week and to incorporate new strategies for harmonious living. By creating a special time devoted to the health of their families, they also created an increased consciousness around sharing and working together.

Children of faculty members (about 10 percent of the student population) sometimes adopted a sense of entitlement, both at school and at home. Leslie's early years (grades one through three) were happy and carefree. By grade four, however, a dark side to Leslie's nature appeared. Fortunately Leslie's bond with Toni was strong. Toni had an informal conference with Leslie's mother Patty, one of our art teachers, telling her that although she (Toni) loved Leslie, she couldn't stand to be around her. She added that Patty had raised a child that only a mother could love—willful, dark, and stubborn. Leslie's resistence was most pronounced in art when she was in class with her mother; she refused to complete any project, fumbling and procrastinating in an area where she had previously shown great talent. Toni added that Leslie's energy was often high, but any disappointment or criticism left her completely deflated. Sometimes Leslie loved to hang around adults; sometimes she had to go off and sulk. Patty was actually relieved to hear the "bad" news. She knew in the back of her mind that life with her daughter had, indeed, become hellish. But little changed until grade six.

In grade five, Leslie's two greatest wishes came true; she gained a father when her mother met and married Craig, and she received, as well, a horse of her own. Yet, Leslie became more willful, refusing to help out, except to take care of her horse. She often had no energy for anything else. In our school conference, her parents and her teachers all agreed that it was not productive for her to stay at The Well. Unless her attitude totally changed, she would not be invited back for the fall semester.

That spring we had altered our attendance policy since so many parents were taking their kids out of school for vacations during the school year. The ruling: No vacations unless the student was sick or there was an emergency. As a result, the trip out west that Craig and Leslie had planned was canceled and Leslie had a tantrum and pulled further into herself. Craig was upset and asked Leslie to think of all the blessings she could and write a list. The task proved long and tedious, but Leslie lighted up a bit.

Leslie had been signed up for a summer session at Pony Farm, which included both riding instruction and the care of horses. Her parents decided to offer her a choice: Attend the Pony Farm or choose to return to The Well in the fall, after a summer devoted to academic work under the direction of a tutor—if Jay accepts you back. All entitlements would end. Despite her love for horses, Leslie chose to forsake Pony Farm and do the academic work. She put her heart into the tutoring and started to run each day to increase her energy. She helped around the house. Near the end of the summer, Toni and I met with Leslie, Patty, and Craig, and I agreed that Leslie could return to The Well in September. During Leslie's final years at The Well, she developed an especially warm relationship with both her parents, and at school, she blossomed again and became a strong force in making other students realize the blessings in their life. As was often the case, parents and school worked together to re-establish loving relationships that had once been intimate but had, over time, become fractured.

In some families, roles are so confused that everyone becomes debilitated. A parent may become so separated from his spiritual being, that he or she is regularly sick and exhausted. The father skirts his responsibilities and becomes a sick child, dependent on special attention. Or a physically heathy, insecure parent may suck the energy out of an entire family by expressing uncontrolled, venomous anger. Or a parent chained to his own self-loathing may constantly heap guilt on all around him.

If a parent is unable to function as an adult, one of the children will attempt to assume the adult role, if only to feel responsible for the hell he experiences. That guilt will spawn its own gruesome effects. Whenever children internalize what does not belong to them, they are in danger of becoming passive targets for the abuse of others. Occasionally, however, extreme dysfunction in a parent allows a child to become extremely functional herself, capable and self-reliant, especially if the child does not accept responsibility for the sickness of the parent.

Conferences also shed light on issues around the rights of siblings. For example, a younger child wants to stay up just as late at night as his older sister. From the older sister's point of view the younger sibling is perceived as being in competition with her. The opportunity for harmony was forfeited when contention and rivalry replaced working together. Parental clarity in such cases, restored a sense of unity in family activities, by clearly defining rights and responsibilities.

Conferences also dealt with inflexible expectations of parents. A mother may declare that Johnny is an artist, that his artistic abilities have been evident since he was a toddler. Jimmy, on the other hand, will become a lawyer or financial expert, because he already thinks and argues as a lawyer might. She may advance the abilities she sees by providing separate, special experiences for each of them. What she sees is often based in truth. But many Jimmy's become artists and many Johnny's become stock brokers or financial experts. We attempted to help parents recognize the multiple talents of a child who has been pigeon-holed, and to allow space for a child to demonstrate his full range of abilities.

We asked parents to notice that when a child is determined to become the next great baseball player or performer or horse whisperer, often life itself propels him in another direction. It is trust in our own multi-dimensionality and flexibility, that enables us to adapt when life makes certain choices for us; but first, we must realize our many talents. We suggest, therefore, that children can excel in many areas if they are given the opportunity and reasonable expectations.

Occasionally, the intent of the conference was thwarted; the child was eclipsed because the parents used the time to air their issues with each other, hoping to find a breakthrough in their own relationship, or hoping to find allies among the teachers. In such a situation, we usually suggested another conference when Toni and I could talk with just the parents.

There are two points I want to make here. First, it seems obvious that often in a marriage, couples need input from a neutral party in order to bring insight and simple truth to a relationship that has become mired. Neither partner can see how their own behavior feeds the conflict. Second, there may be a great deal of sadness and pain in family relationships that is never expressed. The unspoken hurt creates alienation and hostility. When it is allowed to be spoken in a safe environment, when it is respectfully heard, everything shifts. With patience, the submerged, forgotten love comes to the surface and heals the pain of the past.

When open communication is avoided or resented, the child often adopts and carries unresolved family issues which negatively impact his health and his ability to learn. Admittedly, when teachers discuss family issues with parents, they enter uncharted waters, but we dared to explore and probe. Otherwise, children remained locked away, bearing the terrible weight of family secrets or unresolved family animosity. While it may have been our general principle to avoid all family wasp nests, we were willing to approach them for the sake of freeing both the children and adults—in spite of a number of notable stings.

Don't get me wrong. We have had wonderful families at The Well. I am so grateful to have had these people in my life, supporting me or criticizing me, or both. And we recognize that every parent does their best. But, so often they do not see other possibilities, or they do not dare to rock the boat, fearing that their love will not survive complete honesty. Few are able to see that their resentment toward their own parents, dating from their childhood, makes clear and open relationships impossible within a new family. Identifying those resentments and completely forgiving one's own parents (who themselves did their best, but often repeated what they had been taught), changes everything. Those parents with the courage to let go of all past grievances do the highest service to their children. They allow freedom and peace to enter the lives of those who surround them.

If only for the sake of their children, we encouraged all parents to attend Life Institute to deal with their past. We provided a brief description of the workshops, run by John Hart, and recounted briefly our experience there.

When Toni and I took the workshop, we were the only couple there. Thirteen others, strangers to us and to each other, had also paid their $650 without having a clue what would happen. Then there were fifteen aides who had already taken the class. They were there to share their insights, to accompany friends they had convinced to take the class, or simply to refresh their understanding of the principles of the class.

John's magic was, in part, due to his ability to tell extremely unflattering stories about his personal past with humor and directness. He introduced himself as the greatest asshole in the universe and challenged others to reveal their own pathetic past. He asked everyone to come out of his isolation and to reveal that which was hardest to expose. Then each of us had the opportunity to tell the class the story of his or her life.

Few of us got very far in our preferred narrative before John, or the aides, or the novices began to ask pointed questions or shared relevant experiences of their own lives. Everyone had permission, it seemed, to be honest with perfect strangers. And though we were just a group of ordinary people, most questions were gems, often shocking the storyteller into realizations about false assumptions that had ruled his or her life. Most inquiries included the questioner admitting to his own foibles and vulnerability, as might happen in any group which prizes honesty. When a moment for forgiving the past presented itself, the situation was often role-played with someone in class chosen by the storyteller.

After the first life story, we were all exhausted by the huge effort needed to walk in someone else's shoes and by sharing heartfelt bits of our own make up. I was extremely apprehensive about how my own turn would go. But one thing was clear: The collective wisdom of this circle of people who had permission to speak their mind was overwhelm-

Take Me Home
Take me home, joy or sadness.
It matters not who carries me
Back to the cradle of my soul.
Take me home, shining trumpet
Or mournful oboe, take me home.
Jay Garland

ing. There was complete focus and total concern, by all of us, for one person's miserable, yet gallant, life. We had bonded and united in love before the first morning was over. Could this be possible?

Although I had presided over many Meetings at school where we all had permission to speak our own truth, and although I had seen countless miracles of love and healing, I was still stunned by the process of adult strangers meeting on neutral ground without judgment or condemnation, using direct truth to mend what had long festered. Most adults work very hard to set up their lives so that nobody is granted permission to be totally honest—not their mate, nor their children, nor their friends. Part of knowing somebody is knowing what criticism they will not tolerate, what tender subjects to avoid. We learn it when we see the flash of anger or the abrupt rigidity that stops a conversation in its tracks.

It was a total gift to have the tables turned so everybody within the group was afforded the opportunity to say what they saw about others. How simple it is to know yourself when you trust and invite others to expose your own blind spots. If one is capable of listening to truth without resentment or anger, then one can receive a lifetime of insight in a few hours. We all live with people who would set us straight in no time if we could convince them that we would exact no revenge.

Often, Toni and I made use of this insight by applying it to our own relationship. Whenever we were able to accept the other person's anger toward us, instead of defending ourselves or pointing out a similar fault in the other, our relationship opened to new possibilities. It seemed the best opportunity to personally end the cycle of blame and retaliation.

The process of group honesty is accelerated when people realize they are seriously stuck in some aspect of their lives and that the longer they continue in the same direction, the farther they are from the kind of relationship they yearn for. There is some perversity in human nature that fully uses its power to prevent the free expression of others so that one remains blind to oneself, blind to the simplest of solutions. Sophocles' *Oedipus Rex* fully illustrates the pattern.

Simple solutions to life's challenges remain invisible to us, because we live under the illusion that we can hide our feelings and thoughts from each other and live more successfully in an isolated state. In doing so, we lose touch with our own being. Our fear and ignorance make our lives more complicated and limit our ability to discover the freedom that comes when we own and accept our imperfections. The tremendous defensive energy we expend daily to build and maintain walls which block out the truth could serve more productive ends.

At one point, about half of the Well parents experienced, through Life Institute, the dismantling or softening of their defensive walls. They understood that an undefended heart protects us from our own duplicities. But at one particular parent supper, the closeness was so intense and palpable that those who had not attended Life Institute were threatened and felt excluded. They had made a conscious choice not to attend that workshop and felt extremely uncomfortable in the presence of others who expressed their closeness. The school community had split apart. In our enthusiasm and joy to be so connected with each other, we had failed to fulfill our own principle of Inclusion.

Whether our choice to downplay the public affection between adults in order to make the outsiders more comfortable was a mistake or not, is still, for me, an open question. The paradox of too much Inclusion evoking a sense of exclusion may not need to be the final result, but just a stage in the process. But my guess is that the stubbornness and pride of those individuals who shun Inclusion will prevail because individuals must always have the right to choose. The importance of Inclusion appeals to our spiritual sense; it can not be legislated.

Whenever Toni and I asked a student to leave the Well because the child undermined the progress of his class over a period of time, the principle of Inclusion was violated in order to preserve the integrity of the school and the individual interest of those students whose learning was compromised by regular disruptions or a series of attempts to undermine trust or flaunt school rules. In retrospect, Toni and I erred most in our judgement when we gave disruptive students too many second chances, when we pushed the principle of Inclusion beyond the ability of students to control their behavior.

No ideal, if pushed to its limit so that it violates one's other ideals, makes sense. Unbridled Individual Freedom can be used to destroy the freedom of others. Truth can be used as a weapon to hurt. Absolute trust of others can lead quickly to abuse. Excessive loyalty can lead to inability to discriminate truth from falsehood. Inclusion, therefore, remained an ideal to be pursued, not an absolute to be worshipped.

The Early Years

What is it that attracts me to the young? When I am with mature people, I feel their rigidities, their tight crystallizations. They have become, at least in my eyes, like the statues of the famous. Achieved. Final.
Anais Nin

What we habitually love and live by will, in due season, bud, blossom and bear fruit.
Bishop Spaling

It is one of the most beautiful compensations in life that no man can sincerely try to help another without helping himself.
Ralph Waldo Emerson

Even in our first year at The Well, the school came together as an extended family. Kids spent the night at school to burn brush piles, their sleeping bags set out near a bonfire. With each feeding of the fire, new conversations revealed new sides to personalities. We were all at school doing many un-school things. In the morning we ate breakfast together, learning to share cooking and cleaning responsibilities. The barrier of school and play melted away. When kids stayed after school to study the stars, first they did some homework, practiced an instrument, played chess, rode ponies, sang and laughed; then they spent time together in awe of the constellations walking across the sky. Eventually some kids rode horses or bicycles to school, arriving early to tend to their beasts or chat, and in the afternoon, leaving late.

It was a wonder to us, and we felt a new gratitude for the warmth between adults and children. The best of what we had experienced in Alaska was clearly evident here in New Hampshire. Our own children gained a respect for and intimacy with other adults and played happily with their kids. And Toni and I often served as parents for scores of children. The separations which we, at first, respected gave way to new, informal ways of being together. When Toni asked, "Who'd like to bake some cookies?" kids gathered in a knot in the kitchen. "Who'd like to make a birthday cake for Kate?" Everyone would.

School and not school ran together, and we had one life, not work life and time off, but one life of goodness. We were awed by a cycle of giving and receiving that never seemed to end.

By the fall of 1969 our enrollment was up to forty students and changes and adjustments were the order of business. In September, we started a play-reading group which included interested students and parents. Once a week after school, in the afternoon and after a dinner which Toni prepared, we read a play out loud (by Shakespeare or Euripides or Shaw), each of us volunteering to read particular parts. I remember watching Toni read with a book balanced on her protruding belly. It must have been October amid the bustle of the school year. I wondered if our life had gotten too busy, whether we had taken on too much. A few days later, Toni gave birth to Alexandra. We knew that the birth of this child would complete our family. Danda, as we called her from the beginning, brought new, dynamic energy as well as new responsibilities.

We were anxious that The Well be inclusive and welcomed students with a wide range of interests and talents. We were ready to give them the support they needed to share their skills and talents. We wanted to break the mold of acknowledging just those kids who earned A's or those who exhibited model behavior. We knew that doing well on tests or following the rules was a small portion of genuine education, and that being rewarded for being "good" restricted both creativity and expression. We wanted to recognize those children who took risks, those who gave to others in the community, and those who were willing to tell the truth even if it put them in an uncomfortable position. We wanted to recognize children who brought joy into our miniature world, who searched for truth, who loved life, and who took care of animals or plants. We wished to acknowledge those who expressed original thoughts, who possessed uncommon talents, who helped take care of the environment, who exhibited genuine curiosity, or who expressed a highly developed consciousness.

We wanted The Well to accommodate and nourish a wide variety of children, even those who had never liked school before or had low self-esteem. Our vision included assisting students to be multi-dimensional—capable of expressing various sides of their nature, instead of being restricted by a limited identity based on a single talent. We had seen too many schools with cliques of jocks, nerds, and losers who clung together for security on the basis of one shared trait.

Fully developed people have many facets to their nature which change according to who they are with or what they are pursuing. The term, "Renaissance Man," refers to people who express competence and confidence in a variety of venues. Apparently, it was more common during the Renaissance to encourage individuals to play a number of roles. We wanted a school that fostered the same diversity of expression for our students. If one develops self-esteem and a love for self-expression, there is no reason why one can't be a sports enthusiast, a great sculptor, a dancer, *and* an outstanding intellect.

If one is young or young at heart, the same discipline and passion that leads one to be a skillful dancer, can lead one to excel in many other fields. One can be a carpenter and a musician and a film critic. When a school encourages students to excel in a variety of endeavors—a process which begins by deciding to love everything in one's life—students are able to develop multiple outlets for their talents, multiple ways to express themselves. Theater productions invite all to be (at least for the duration of the play), someone new and different, to express not the limited self, but the greater self.

Flexibility is a virtue because increased consciousness demands that we change our identity often, always expanding who we are and what we know. When teachers are able to play and learn as children do, and when children can teach others from their inner authority, it is time to celebrate.

At first we did not give report cards to the students. We felt that the immense significance most parents gave to report cards, grades, and tests, had a limiting effect on children. We gave plenty of tests and quizzes in order for teachers and students to understand what students had mastered and what they had not, but those tests did not culminate in report card grades. But after several years, it was evident that our graduates experienced a difficult transition to schools that were highly grade conscious. Our students had not mastered the process of honing in on what produced good grades.

After the first two years, we decided to issue report cards for students above grade four. The report would include grades in specific subjects and subjective evaluations in a number of areas: attitude towards learning, attitude toward teachers, willingness to assume responsibility, leadership abilities, helpfulness to others, ability to work with others, effectiveness in daily jobs, and effectiveness in communication.

Although this amended report card worked well, it still failed to register the scores of ways in which students contributed to the functioning and success of our program and enriched the lives of everyone. So we adopted an open-ended award system with engraved plaques to be kept in school and paper awards to go home with the students.

The awards,were varied and addressed qualities and accomplishments that we valued at The Well. Here is a sampling of our awards:

School Friend	Bringing Joy to Others
Brilliant Original Poet	Persistence
Essay Writing	Great Artist
Poetry Recital	Leadership
Music Performance	Kindness
Joy in Music	Adaptability
French Conversation	Joyous Laughter
Latin Translator	Skilled Outdoorsman
Spanish Guru	Wit
Russian Wizard	Deep Thinker
Guiding Light to Others	Baker for Coffee Houses
Enthusiasm	Responsibility
Scientific Curiosity	Clearing the Pond for Hockey
Mythology Wonder	Being a Light in the Classroom
Conscientiousness in Homework	Original Thinker
Excellent in All-Around Academics	Grace in Dancing
Compassion for Others	Follow Through
Reliable Grounds Keeper	Concentrated Drawing
Right-hand Man	Expressive Drawing
Right-Hand Woman	Willingness to Take a Risk
Being a Great Morning Greeter to Others	Honesty
Consciousness of the World's People	Metamorphosis
Delight in Learning	Perceptiveness
Innovation	Personal Growth

Depth of Inquiry	The Glue of your Class
Putting Others at Ease	Expressive Singing
Gentleness	Expert at Stacking Wood
Amazing Awareness	Basketball Giant
Compassion	Relentless, Courageous Soccer Play
Being There for Others	Dynamic Sculptor
Extending Self	Batik Genius
Standing Up for Others	Painting with Acrylics
Friend to Young People	Concentration in Yoga
Doctor Doolittle	Teaching Others
Drama	Passing in Hockey
Courageous Defense in Soccer	Most Improved in Math
Team Player	Going the Extra Mile

The awards were always tailored to fit the individual. Yet, they represented qualities that benefitted The Well, qualities that teachers valued in their students, and qualities that students valued in each other.

For me, it is a spiritual duty of teachers to discover the genius in every child, even the ones that may be the most annoying. If I cannot discover and express the greatness in others and keep those gifts in the forefront of my mind each day, then I do not meet the requirements of being an authentic teacher. Individuals are often the last to discover their talents; many people need to have their great qualities pointed out regularly before they can accept them as real. It is in knowing our greatness that we realize our spiritual dimensions and gain self-esteem. One who lacks self-esteem is extremely reluctant to express himself. Although self-esteem can not be taught, it can be encouraged by praising the outstanding qualities latent in our fellow beings.

Those adults and children who possess considerable self-esteem and awareness bind a community together. They are naturals at welcoming and including others. They have no need to mete out abuse in reaction to abuse they have endured. They break the chain of the punitive cycle which runs according to old tribal law and ensures that abuse never ends: an eye for an eye, a tooth for a tooth, a concept which, unfortunately, makes great sense to some children.

Including New Teachers

During the first years of The Well, we added more and more new teachers who could enrich our program. Thrilled with the progress of their kids, a number of parents wanted to be more involved in the school and share in the life of their children. The extraordinary talent that existed within the parent body allowed the school to provide an ever richer program. When the school quickly grew in numbers, we needed new teachers to share the load. We looked first at the parent body.

When we looked at the qualities of teachers, we looked for people who could see the greatness in children. We wanted givers, nurturers, and life-long learners. We looked for people who had enough self-esteem to take criticism gracefully, who already had an interest in becoming more aware, and who were generally open to life. Such teachers can not only teach; they can learn from everyone and everything, from difficulties as well as from what comes easily, from adults, and, especially from children. They serve as role models gifted in the ability to learn.

Often a child will tell a teacher who is experiencing a moment of self-doubt, "You can ski this trail. I'll go with you," or "I love your painting." A child who has not been invited to a birthday party often has the wisdom to say, "They can't invite everybody." Their acceptance of the situation helps to relieve the teacher who assumed the child's heart was broken. When a child questions a teacher about what she just wrote on the board, "Couldn't that have been written better?" the child gives a wonderful gift. There are opportunities for teachers to learn from students every day. Any teacher who can graciously take as

> Few people even scratch the surface, much less exhaust the contemplation of their own experiences ... For the weakness of experience is that it so soon gets stereotyped; without new situations and crisis it becomes so conventional as to be practically unconscious. Very few people get any really new experience after they are twenty-five, unless there is a real change in environment. Most older men live only in the experience of their youthful years.
>
> **Randolph Ralph Bourne**

> See a great fire, how the flames pass from shape to shape, lambent and aspirant flames, poised or waving, some open like fully-blown tulips and some, pursed to a point like shut daisies, but all vanishing as soon as formed and none recurring just as it was. All experience burns away like that.
> **C.E. Montagne**

> In the person who is open to experience each stimulus is freely relayed through the nervous system, without being disturbed by any process of defensiveness.
> **Carl R. Rogers**

well as generously offer, exemplifies the life process of reciprocal giving and receiving which is so necessary for a gentle community.

We asked all our parents to share what they loved with groups of students. Fritz Wetherbee, the father of one of our students, Caleb, provided a figure drawing class which made kids much more comfortable illustrating the stories they read. Later Fritz orchestrated a movie with the kids, teaching them how to think through a simple story line, transforming the intent of each scene into a series of shots. He taught them to position and use the camera so that it became totally their movie. They made *The Chase* with the simplest of plots. An initial confrontation led to a chase, and as the chase proceeded, more and more people joined in. It started with two people running through the picnic ground where two lovers were gorging themselves. Others joined the chase as they passed through the woods, into downtown Peterborough, in and out of the doughnut shop, down the highway, and finally, up Pack Monadnock Mountain to the very top. Watching the film, it looked like all the older kids were running non-stop for hours—all well-conditioned marathon runners. We were all very proud of it.

Later students made *The New Kid*, a story of a new student who arrives at school only to be held at bay by the school dog. This poor kid undergoes a series of traumatic experiences, and finally, he is happily adopted into the school family. The film helped to address a real situation created by our possessive Saint Bernard who protected the original group of students from any new students who joined The Well. Unfortunately, when Camel starting biting, we had to put him down, unsettling many kids. Acting out The New Kid helped us all to deal with the loss.

Patsy Wilkins, another teacher with two daughters at The Well offered a nature-based art class. She took students for walks to gather materials to incorporate into art treasures which were then displayed around the school.

Katy Barnes, the first parent to join our full-time staff also had two children at The Well. The energy that she brought to every aspect of the school lifted us up. She taught kindergarten, first, or second grade for seventeen years. She helped build, she played soccer. She taught weaving, knitting, contra-dancing, and singing. She cleaned and vacuumed after school or on weekends. When you work with someone who is willing to do everything, you have a true partner.

Two other parents whose two sons attended The Well, brought a high level of music to our youngsters. Jim Bolle taught violin and viola to individual students for weeks and then brought them together in an ensemble in a matter of minutes while we watched and listened in wonder. Jocelyn Bolle brought part singing to The Well and taught our first chorus. We had seen the wonderful effect of singing when we visited The Meeting School, a Quaker high school, in nearby Rindge. We decided to include a lot of singing at The Well. We sang rounds, madrigals, and musicals, and chorus became a regular class at The Well. Those two fine parents also founded Monadnock Music. For thirty-five years, Monadnock Music provided the finest music in New Hampshire, drawing in artists from all over the country and abroad to give a long series of performances each summer.

Another Well parent, Widdie Iselin, helped with cleaning and organizing. Later she taught kids to speak French with an authoritative accent. She also served as a first-class angel for me and brought me all kinds of interesting books, including the remarkable *A Course in Miracles* which changed my thinking about how I wanted to lead my life and how I wanted to teach.

Carol Whitehouse, whose four children of her own, a nephew who needed some direction, and two other children whom she and her husband "adopted" and tuitioned into school, became an amazing reading teacher and then a most resourceful classroom teacher for fifteen years. Her love of literature, poetry, music, horses, birds, and play brightened our days. She and her husband, Brooks, built a house within a stone's throw of the school and dedicated one of the rooms for our use as a classroom. While their house was under construction, her family moved in with ours. Those were among the happiest of our days at The Well. Together, our two families had so much life, so much talent, so much joy, it is a wonder that we ever lived apart. During their stay with us and through all the years they lived in their new house, Brooks regularly commuted three to four hours a day to hold down a job in Boston to support his family-and-a-half.

Gundy Khouw, mother of three Well students, a woman with no fears, picked up the teaching of French, and lead trips to Quebec and Paris so the kids would experience the full richness of French culture. For twenty years she sewed and altered hundreds of costumes for our productions, never asking for or expecting help. Her spirit lifted us each time she undertook a new adventure for herself, traveling about the globe, learning the skills of welding and fly fishing, taking care of people in need, working for her husband Dave, and raising her three children while running their farm/household.

Betsy Nields, a nurse by profession, a musician by avocation, and mother of three children at The Well, taught a generation of kids to read—and read incredibly well—in first grade. With all the enthusiasm of a kid, she brightened and ordered our flower gardens, sang in our choruses, wrote plays for the children, and took over from Gundy the making of creative costumes for our productions. These were only a few of the wonderful teachers we were fortunate to have at the Well.

During the first year of the high school, three students moved into our house as unofficial, non-paying, boarding students. Once again our family was extended, enriched by the high energy and the many talents of those three boys.

For me, the two years of having a high school were like an emotional, exhilarating, and exhausting roller coaster ride. As I see it now, I made critical mistakes hiring some of the new teachers. I opted, for the most part, for highly intelligent, highly successful teachers with great academic credentials, assuming they would magically adopt the culture of a school based on Inclusion and community. Only well into the second year of the high school did I realize that the faculty was strongly divided over how to go about educating high school students. The news came out in a Meeting. A few students wanted an explanation of the "shit list," a term for what they intuitively perceived as a faculty attitude that the highly academically qualified, high-achieving students were welcome at the school, and those who were not were rejected and judged to be inferior and hopeless as students. As it turned out, there was strong agreement among a group of teachers who thought it was inappropriate to mix fine students with struggling ones. From my point of view, the combination had provided a wonderful, productive, chemistry. But, I had to acknowledge, we had reached a crisis point.

Also, the culture which supported open Meetings where anything was up for discussion, was anathema to this same group of teachers who wanted to call the shots, maintain clear authority, and make all significant decisions. They also felt their authority was being undermined by the many meetings I chaired in order to get the input of the parents of high school students to explain what we were doing in the high school and to explore other alternatives. These same teachers felt betrayed by discussing what, according to them, should be mandated by them.

When the students assumed there must be a blackball list, they correctly identified, one by one, which students were deemed to be unsuitable by the teachers who wanted only good students. I was shocked by how deeply we were divided, how I had not seen what the students clearly saw. I compounded my first mistake by announcing that The Well would return the following year with only grades one through nine. The high school at The Well would close. And so it did. A remnant of the school survived in a new location and called itself The Van School; it lasted for one year. Ironically, this school included members of the "shit list" and the same faculty members who wanted to exclude them. Such is life.

In retrospect, I saw that our high school held such great potential, and I deeply regretted that I had allowed it to die. The learning that transpired through our high school, for all the exclusive thoughts by a few of its teachers, was phenomenal for the twenty-four students involved. The most astounding growth was apparent in the former dropouts who produced breathtaking art work. They also excelled in writing, literature, psychology, geometry, and in general artistic courage and talent. It was not unusual for the drawing and sculpture students to voluntarily work from 3:30 until 9:00 in the evenings. The few graduates from twelfth grade were admitted to the selective colleges of their choice. Only the state college of the University of New Hampshire (UNH) refused to recognize credits from our non-accredited program and rejected one of our students.

The closing of our high school made me realize, more than ever, the importance of matching teachers, who themselves experience life primarily through their heart, with parents and students committed to the primacy of heart-based education. My own relationships with our high school students had helped me to grow personally. Looking back, I see we did have a nucleus of great teachers with which to rebuild a harmonious and exceptional high school program. My own blindness and a broken heart precluded taking timely action to refashion what already had seeds of greatness. I grieved its loss.

Experience seems to be like the shining of a bright lantern. It suddenly makes clear in the mind what was already there, perhaps, but dim.
Walter De La Mare

Admissions

We have never been selective about taking new students. We never ask for records or grades or accomplishments before accepting a student. We did, however, reserve the right to place students in classes where they were comfortable and could do their best. We've taken many students that were labeled by other schools, as having severe mental, emotional, or physical disabilities, because we thought the school and community could benefit by their contributions.

For us, what best predicted the success of a student who entered The Well was the nature and personality of the mother. Mothers who were flexible and loved to learn with their children, who themselves longed to be students again, mothers without an agenda of their own of what must happen for their children, mothers who wanted the inner nature of their children to be nurtured, boded a happy and long relationship. The ones that reeked of discontent or tended to blame other schools for their child's lack of success predicted trouble. But we accepted their children, anyway, if the mothers were willing to abide by the requirements of the The Well.

Although we never put academic achievement at the top of our list of priorities, we were, nevertheless, very proud of the academic accomplishments of our students. For the most part, our students have exceeded all expectations, because they came to believe in their ability to succeed. The high academic achievement of our students (our graduates who opt for boarding schools usually applied to the most academically competitive schools, and conservatively speaking, over 75 percent of those applications received letters of acceptance) is not, in

Success

Success is counted sweetest
By those who ne'er succeed.
To comprehend the nectar
Requires the sorest need.

Not one of all the purple host
Who took the flag to-day
Can tell the definition,
So clear of victory,

As he, defeated, dying,
On whose forbidden ear
The distant strains of triumph
Break, agonized, and clear.

Emily Dickinson

our opinion, just due to superior academic teaching.

It is, instead, a by-product of a community built on decency, respect, and trust which allows students to express their genius in a wide range of academic and non-academic activities. A student who opts to mow the grass during his lunch hour gains respect in his own eyes and in the eyes of others. He will, therefore, improve academically. A student who pursues theater will, therefore, improve academically. A student who helps create a school newspaper during his free time will improve academically. A student who joins an after-school math class will also improve academically. The fact is, students reveal more and more intelligence the more they do what they love to do.

Over the years, the students who chose to do the most were usually the happiest and the most successful, both academically and in terms of their personal growth. Their energy moved outward and embraced everything and everybody in their environment. As in every field of endeavor, positive energy flow creates health, intelligence, and well-being. When that flow becomes habitual, genius begins to reveal itself in many guises. It is a universal principle that love expands possibilities within and without.

What one has not experienced, one will never understand in print.
Isadora Duncan

The man who thoroughly enjoys what he reads or does, or even what he says, or simply what he dreams or imagines, profits to the full. The man who seeks to profit through one form of discipline or another, deceives himself.

Henry Miller

Occasionally, when a student flourishes, one or both parents freak out. This occurs because the child, no longer limited by fear, breaks the bounds of what is considered acceptable behavior in his family, and no longer fits the mold that a parent required. It is not that she becomes rude or surly, but now she may express freely what the parents want hidden. She may no longer limit her love or approval to those within the family, because her definition of family has grown. Or she may shed a negative self image which, for some reason, the family still depends on.

When parents removed a child from The Well before he or she

graduated, it was often during a time when the child was experiencing accelerated growth and a new openness to friends and adults. There was a breakthrough into expanded learning and self-reliance, into new freedoms of expression. There was a willingness to confront old issues around negativity and to chart a new course. The newness of it all caught some parents unprepared, and they resisted the change by pulling their child out of The Well.

Over the years, other parents withdrew children because they thought that our expectations for students were too high or that we gave too much homework. They were often right. When parents declared that our expectations were excessive, their children got the message that they could never do what we were asking. So the parents' belief in the inability of the child to make a breakthrough nullified our belief that they could. In that case, belief in limitations won out.

We had a system that usually worked. We asked parents to prevent students from doing homework for more than the designated limit for their grade level. They could write a note letting us know their child had reached the time limit. We asked students to tell their classroom teacher whenever their homework surpassed a time limit for a particular grade. For seventh-graders the maximum time allowed was one and one-half hours. Our purpose was to have students adopt strategies that would economize the time spent on homework. We didn't want students to procrastinate or to allow their homework to consume all their family time at home. When two students reported to their teacher that they had reached or exceeded the limit, the teacher would reduce the homework assignments. If it were only one student, the teacher would use her own judgment.

Inclusion through Soccer

For almost thirty years, our school has had one or more school soccer teams. While a lot of the kids loved a variety of sports, and many played in recreational leagues in their local towns, The Well School treated soccer as the official school sport. Although we enjoyed playing many other sports on campus (especially hockey, basketball, and ultimate frisbee) in an informal way, soccer enjoyed a special place.

Soccer, by its very nature, required a large group of kids and depended on those kids working together. Kindergarten children often learned the game in an informal atmosphere by playing with multiple age groups and their teachers. For the youngest kids we focused on full participation, the joy of running, and the challenge of controlling the ball. Their teachers, happy to be included in the game, encouraged passing and working together.

Starting with grade five, the focus shifted to improving basic skills, learning the responsibilities of each position, and learning group strategies for offense and defense. Our basic, everyday drills were designed to improve kicking power, trapping, heading the ball, passing with give-and-goes, throw-ins, scoring techniques, playing the goalie position, and above all, how to play effective defense within the rules of the game.

We played during September and October. Traditionally, we practiced a full hour at a time, three days a week, during regular school hours. We practiced on our beautiful, regulation soccer field. (One of our parents and teachers masterminded and helped build the field.) Soccer was a required class for all students in grades five through eight. Games were held after school and were optional, but most students participated when their schedule allowed.

Learning one team sport prepared them well for many other team sports, especially basketball, hockey, lacrosse, field hockey—games of continual action until an infraction stopped the clock. A good soccer player who mentally understood offensive and defensive strategy easily transferred that understanding to other team sports.

Because everyone participated in soccer, even those not inclined to play sports, it was a team-building activity which asked all, beginners and experienced players alike, to participate fully. The daily focus in practice was, therefore, on individual improvement in a particular aspect of the game, such as kicking with more force and accuracy and trapping lofted balls. We taught strategies to make the team more effective, both offensively and defensively.

Those who feared contact with other players or feared being struck by a ball, tended to run away from the action as a tactic for self-preservation. Oddly enough, these were the players who suffered the most injuries. From their perspective, the game resembled combat more than recreation. To break the cycle of fear, we taught them how to make contact without causing injuries to themselves, and we practiced safe contact techniques as one of our regular drills. Some of the most timid quickly gained confidence when playing soccer with their classmates and friends during scrimmages, but they reverted to their old, fearful style in games when their opponents were strangers. Sometimes in the short term, it was hard to see definite progress, but over a period of years, everyone learned to enjoy the game and to trust their ability to play aggressively without getting hurt.

Our first two years were a trial. As a group, the boys refused to be inclusive; they only wanted to pass to their best friends and rarely, if ever, passed to a girl. They refused to recognize anyone who hadn't proved, to their satisfaction, that they could be trusted to move the ball effectively down field. Reasoning with these boys rarely remedied the situation. Repeatedly removing them from a game each time they ignored a member of their team had a greater effect. Eventually, they realized that the success of the team rested with the defensive skills of the girls (most girls preferred playing defense), and that a number of the girls were, in fact, trustworthy and skillful as offensive soccer players.

Once, the opponent's coach, whose large middle school team was awed by the skillful playing of our girls, shouted to his male players on the field, "Those aren't girls, they're soccer players. Get aggressive." Whenever our own team players shared that perspective, our team melded beautifully.

Despite the obstacles it presented, our soccer teams were coed by design. We needed everybody to play; we needed everyone to practice. But it was difficult to find other coed teams to play against, so for the most part, over a thirty year period, we played all-boys teams.

We experienced, in the course of the years, some clearly definable periods of soccer. Originally we played public schools with boys teams. At first, we were outclassed, especially by large schools which included older kids, a few of whom could drive and shave, as well as play soccer. The inherent physical dominance of an uncoordinated giant, more or less out of control, bearing down on one of our female players, caused her, at first, to lose all courage.

Our challenge, initially, was mental. Before each game our players would look over the players on the opposition and quake. When our comparatively young, small, skinny players saw the rugged, athletic, trees they were about to face, they lost their heart before the game had even begun.

In addition, boys traditionally have the attitude that they are innately superior to girls at sports, which gave our all-male opponents the added motivation to trounce us; otherwise they experienced a humbling at the least, but more likely a genuine humiliation. Our team had the challenge to prove that girls can hold their own with boys and that boys and girls can work together to complement each other.

In our very first soccer game, we lost four girls to injuries, and had to carry the poor victims, one at a time, off the field of battle. The game seemed to go on forever. Virginia, one of the survivors, later that night over dinner recounted the game to her father, telling him we had done well in our first real soccer game.

"What was the score?" Richard inquired.

"Eleven to one," Virginia answered proudly.

"You won?" Her father was impressed. He knew the dynamics of athletics from his youth.

"No, we lost, but we really did well. Only four kids got hurt."

This humiliating experience taught us a lot about our weaknesses.

It also awakened the full force of my competitive spirit which had lain dormant since my high school basketball days. Although I had never played soccer as a kid, I saw that the principles of basketball, especially the principles of playing defense, were applicable to soccer.

We practiced defense and more defense, learning to mirror an opponent, learning to position ourself opposite the ball, learning to close down on the opponent as he approached the goal, learning to stay exactly between the opponent's dominant foot and the goal that was behind one's back, and learning to direct the movement of an opponent so that he had to shoot at a bad angle. The warning was always the same: Don't go for the ball. Over the next three weeks we lost six games, but the scores indicated that we were becoming competitive.

We practiced when to attack and when to back off. We learned how not to be duped by an opposing player, and how to give space to the opponent depending on his speed, his ability to control the ball, and his distance from our goal. We got tougher once we realized that by having an intelligent defense, we could slow the opponent's attack to a crawl. All of us, working together, could frustrate our opponents. The hard work (often after practice we had to jump in the pond to cool off) paid off.

Most boys love to play offense and seek the recognition which comes from scoring goals. This makes them aggressive, selfish, and very predictable. They have a hard time understanding that the techniques they used at age eight (repeatedly using the same fake, dribbling around one opponent after another until one has a clear shot) does not work against older teams. It is, however, in accord with human nature, that when a tactic doesn't work, to use it more, to try harder and even harder, and then in frustration, to fall down and claim you've been kicked and complain that the referee didn't call it. And then, you rise up, and go back to the same failed strategy.

One boy in ten just loves to run. He not only plays aggressive offense, but he chases and plays defense the length of the field. These dogged boys are invaluable on a team and disrupt the composure of the rival team. And then there is the boy that hardly runs at all and positions himself just in the right spot and scores with little effort.

The girls that became awesome defensive players actually heard what their insightful coach (Did I tell you I was the coach?) repeated and learned to play defense by following a few simple principles. They might have had little natural athletic ability, but with experience, their judgment sharpened. After a few minutes into the game, they had sized up which opponents to pester and which to retreat from so that, at the crucial moment, they could use their bodies to block a shot. These girls, who took pride in their guts and their smarts, took unfair advantage of their opponents by being exactly at the right place at the crucial moment and made the boys pay for their lack of imagination and their lack of teamwork.

The utter frustration our girls induced in the opposition made them the target for dirty paybacks. So we practiced the legal use of the shoulder a lot. They learned to collide safely when they ran into my 200-plus-pound frame; they timed their contact to achieve the maximum effect á la martial arts. They learned to pummel me and enjoy it. So in the end, when a boy attempted to flatten a seemingly fragile, harmless girl, he got a rude awakening and had his teeth jarred.

Of course a girl loves to use her power whenever she sees the let's-hurt-them-if-we-can't-win-legitimately look in an opponent's eye.

That look calls forth the kind of measured courage needed to educate the bully. During scrimmages the girls repeatedly earned respect from the boys on their own team as well.

When money for school athletics dried up in our area in the late '80s and early '90s, and the only school teams were those of the large consolidated schools, we joined a recreational league centered in our town that sponsored one league for fifth- and sixth-graders, and another for seventh-, eighth-, and ninth-graders. Except for one year, the oldest players we fielded were in eighth grade, which proved to be a challenge. Most opposing teams were composed of kids who loved to play soccer but had been cut from their school teams. Two other school teams (private schools in the area) also joined the League, but we were the only real coed group. Our girls on the field usually outnumbered our boys.

We upset a lot of locals by winning too often. Over a number of years, the charges leveled at us became more pointed. The recreation commission invited us to a meeting to explain that we had an unfair advantage. We practiced too much! Too many of our parents attended the game and they cheered too loudly (our parents were loud, but fair; they often cheered for the skill or grit of the opponents, as well as for our own players). Many games were played on our field (never the playoffs, however). They claimed the referees that we provided favored our team. They made these charges despite the fact that the league used our field because they had a shortage of fields, and they had asked us to supply and pay the refs for home games, because they couldn't find enough. Often, at a game downtown, no referee would show up, and, after asking the other team if they could provide a referee, we would solicit referees from among our parents. In my perception, our referees were more than fair. If not, my sense of justice dictated that they would never again referee for our team.

For years, we were obviously an unwanted thorn in the hide of the league. During one game, one of our girls was viciously injured by an older player on the opposite team who was rumored to be a tenth-grader that had been kicked off his high school team after the season started. I was angry and asked for him to be taken off the field. The coach refused. I had no hard evidence about his status. Later I called the high school to confirm the rumor, and I notified the soccer commission that this large overage, illegal player was a danger to the younger kids. They refused to bar him from playing.

Here's how bad it got. Early in the next soccer season, our fifth- and sixth-grade team played a team coached by the new president of the league. We provided the referee. When the referee called off sides against their team, awarding us a free kick, this president-coach ran onto the field, picked up the ball, stopped the game, and commenced yelling at the referee.

I ran out on the field only to have him yell at me that it was against the rules of the league to call off sides in a game, and that if we wanted to play in such an aggressive way, we should join another league. Why didn't we follow the rules provided by the league? We were obviously trying to gain unfair advantage, and he, as president of the league, wasn't going to allow it.

I told him as long as we had been in the league we had always played with the off-side rule. He said that was a total lie. I produced the current list of the rules recently published by the recreation commission in which, among its other rules, it spelled out the off-side rule. His anger roared; he was over the top. At the end of the season we were barred from playing recreational soccer again.

We had hoped that the recreational league would allow us to make contact with other local children and create new friendships for our kids. It accomplished nothing of the kind. We hoped the community would see that our children were not arrogant because they went to a private school, but that they found utter joy in the game and played fairly. Instead, we were hated for our competence.

The next year, we traveled long distances to find school teams to play. I had forgotten how pleasant and hospitable school teams were. The pit-bull mentality of the recreational league was nowhere in evidence. In fact, in one game where we could only field ten players, the other team lent us their best player, the coach's son.

Soccer brought so much joy to the students that it became a regular pastime, a regular avenue to release energy and have fun. The one-hour lunch time was often devoted to casual pick-up games. It was not uncommon to see on one side of the field, a furious soccer game in progress, while on the other, kids were doing cart wheels and socializing. It brought boys and girls together and introduced mutual respect into the nature of their relationships.

Often, children from all eight grades would play together during the lunch hour. At these times, the older ones took great care not to harm the smaller kids. Aware of the difficulty of playing against bigger, rougher players, they selectively backed off and slowed down whenever a young player was near. It was an unspoken, unwritten law, a code of conscience, to make allowances for age, experience, size, weight, and skill level.

Older students showed younger ones how to handle a ball. They asked the younger kids to shoot while they played goalie and then celebrated the goals as if they had made the score themselves. In such a way, even relatively uncoordinated older students, playing as tenderly and lovingly as a father might with his child, became heroes for their younger counterparts, not because of their macho, athletic exhibitions, but because of their compassion and love.

Soccer was a way to relax. When graduates visited The Well, as they did on many occasions, soccer served as a vehicle for them to reconnect with our students and former teachers. The graduates enjoyed testing their skills against ours. Soccer had the power to create a sacred circle where all were welcome.

In fact, the therapeutic value of soccer was so great that there were many Saturday or Sunday games at the Well between mixed groups of parents and students. It was not uncommon during Thanksgiving weekends and the final months of the school year for graduates, students, and faculty to come together to play soccer. What can be more joyful than the mixing of age groups doing something together they love.

Built into our school calendar each fall was what we called Wood Day, a Saturday morning when the entire community gathered to cut, haul, split, and stack wood for the stoves that heated several class-rooms. Parents and teachers brought chainsaws, axes, trucks, and wood splitters. Many dragged branches into huge brush piles. Wood Day also included sprucing up garden plots and planting bulbs all over the open spaces on campus. Not until we had worked for three hours, did we break for lunch.

After changing clothes, the parents and students gathered for a soccer game (I always played with the students). While many parents preferred to watch, there were always some who loved the challenge of playing against the kids (including their own) whose grit and skill they had admired during our soccer season.

Parents, with or without soccer experience, loved to play. When they became frustrated or winded, they often resorted to grabbing, holding a kid's shirts or pants, shoving, elbowing or tripping. The kids loved it. It was a tacit acknowledgment of how far the children had come.

In our life together at The Well, we stressed qualities that promoted Community: treating others with respect; expressing one's thoughts and feelings; being vulnerable; developing a positive attitude; communicat-ing from one's heart; negotiating differences; and practicing inclusion, compassion, and gentleness. When we began competitive sports, we were slaughtered, degraded, and injured. In the rough and tumble world where the mentality of might makes right prevails, we were unable to stand up for ourselves physically, emotionally, and mentally.

Soccer was one route to learning how to be strong in situations where attempts at decency and respect were trampled, where large bodies could be intimidating weapons, and where violence was often rewarded. We were a small school with relatively young children for their grade levels; our students would never be older, bigger, stronger, or more athletic then their opponents. Nevertheless, they had to learn to mix it up physically. But especially, they needed to learn that intelligence and teamwork between the sexes could compensate for what they lacked physically. In the end they were not just a good team; they were a team united by their spirit and willingness to work together in order to slay Goliath.

So many of our players developed a real passion for soccer, even those who were new to the game or who did not see themselves as athletes. They knew that each year we had to focus and dedicate ourselves to be competitive. Therefore, they submitted to becoming disciplined soccer players, not just disciplined students. Their pride in their accomplishment was matched only by the pride of their parents and the pride of their coach.

The Integration of Grades

We found it important, from time to time, to integrate the students from several classrooms into a greater whole. Since each classroom tended to operate with its own separate agenda, and students within each classroom often separated into groups or cliques, it was easy for all of us to lose sight of our goal of an integrated school community. Occasionally, we broke up set friendships or brought grades together to create a greater mix of relationships and to form a single, dynamic culture.

When fifth-, sixth-, seventh-, or eighth-graders devoted an hour of their lunch time each week to take care of the kindergarten class while their teacher had a break, the cross fertilization created an array of new beauty within The Well. When an older student read to a younger child, there was something more important than reading going on. When a person from one grade pushed the swing for a member of another grade, it was a not just swinging; it was a widening of personal worlds. When students from one class presented their projects to other classes, magic happened. When multi-grades played together at lunch, divisions melted away and everyone belonged to a larger whole, a larger family.

Consider the alternative. Isolated classrooms produce isolated students. We live at a time when students and children are already too isolated because they are watching hours of television, wearing headsets while listening to their own music, playing video games, or losing themselves in a computer program. They often eat on the run, without any meaningful family contact, and then they are isolated in same-age peer groups (grades or classes) six to eight hours a day. It is entirely unnatural to be cooped up with others at approximately the same stage of development.

We had learned of the drawbacks of separating kids by age when we worked at a boarding school in Deerfield, Massachusetts. One of our duties was to monitor a dormitory with fifteen thirteen-year-old girls, keeping them busy so, according to school policy, they wouldn't have any free time to get into trouble. Despite our best efforts, there was little balance or perspective or sanity in that dormitory. Every little daily drama was magnified and intensified by these highly hormonal girls. A pair of lost socks created panic, hysteria, and eventually confrontation, screaming, and inconsolable crying. When things finally calmed down, a single glance could propel things back into high-intensity drama with jealous altercations and broken hearts. The moon seemed to synchronize their moods. If one girl became homesick, everybody became homesick. If one girl was undone by an upcoming test, all were agonizing over it. Keeping kids of the same age together magnified insecurities and created an aura of fear and impending disaster.

School pushes the limits of separation. It removes kids from a wider, more stable society and creates a pent-up nervousness, a general frenzy. It separates kids from society; it isolates students into buildings with few open windows and many shut doors. School can be simply a laboratory where repressed children are kept busy on a variety of treadmills by adults who fear spontaneity and rebellion. Unfortunately, school is mandatory.

Can students, after hours, suddenly come to life and engage in productive activities which expand their horizons? For some, it's the only chance to function with their hearts fully engaged. For others, it's the only chance to express their negativity and loss of hope.

We have been blessed over the years with a number of excellent teachers who were intimately involved with The Well for fifteen or twenty years at a time. These teachers shared their students and their own children with the entire community and gave others in the community the authority to intercede when appropriate, and even to reprimand children who were out of line. We did not consider such intercession a reflection of our own inability to keep control. Instead, we functioned as a community where everyone had equal authority.

But we have also experienced discord within the same community when a teacher creates a private classroom, when he appoints himself king, and then separates himself from community activities. The general harmony yields to struggle and wrangling, even to factions among the other teachers supporting the right for the lone wolf to be a wolf.

When several classes and their teachers are brought together, the switch from the routine of separate class schedules to multi-grade activities causes temporary discomfort. When students and teachers move to a new environment, patterns of old relationships are disrupted. New associations and new bonds form out of the chaos and enrich the experience for everyone who is open to the process.

Each fall for many years, we deliberately moved the older students to Interlocken Camp in Hillsboro, New Hampshire, for a week. There we were hosted by the parents of three of our students, Richard and Susan Herman, the camp directors. We assigned the group of fifth-, sixth-, seventh-, and eighth-graders to five cabins. Each cabin housed two students from each grade and a teacher. By design, group activities during the day also mixed students and exposed students to other kids and teachers. We chose to disturb the regular pattern of relationships in order to further new and different bonds. Within a few hours at camp, people had altered their alignments, permitting themselves an opportunity to discover new friendships and a new appreciation for one another.

At a dance with a large group of children, familiar partnering quickly repeats and reconfigures into old patterns. When the partnerships are changed and one joins with less familiar partners, new ways of dancing and talking occur. At Interlocken, a new orientation dictated a new order of being with people.

We deliberately fostered new friendships because we felt strongly that each child had things to teach every other child. For us, that was the point of being together—to learn from each other. The layout of furniture in a typical classroom symbolizes the power structure of those that use that room. All desks but one face the single, larger desk of the teacher, as if the teacher held all the keys to the kingdom of knowledge. Not for us! It was clear that teachers had much to learn from each child, and each child was a teacher for every other child. Our tactics to artificially throw people together were aimed at furthering that end.

Friendships

Students usually opt for a few close friends, basically ignoring other kids. It's part of the human process to divide mankind into two groups: those we value and want to be with and those we ignore and avoid. The appropriateness of this natural division depends on one's point of view.

From our vantage point, while it is most comfortable to be with the people we favor as often as possible, growth often results from focusing on others, the unfamiliar ones, the uncomfortable ones. Our experience teaches us that growth results from dealing with what is difficult, awkward, hidden, and new.

The shadow side of personality represents the untouchable side of oneself. This darkness is too uncomfortable and threatening to become part of the ego identity and is hidden out of sight and out of mind. Yet, maintaining that part of the self that we never acknowledge and never see requires a tremendous investment of life energy. As long as one remains alienated from one's shadow, this energy lies locked up, unavailable to serve any productive purpose.

Furthermore, by the instinctual, psychological process of projection, one sees one's hidden darkness in others who are not admitted to the inner circle of special friends. One then judges the dark people as bad, stupid or warped, unworthy and untouchable. As the separation of familiar friends from alien outsiders deepens, the need to remain glued to those who cause us no friction intensifies. Cliques are powerful vehicles of separation. Something vital, some strong opportunity for growth, is lost in this search for best friends who seem

Whatever we blame, that you have done yourself.
George Groddeck

to provide permanent safety and comfort, and who protect us from seeing our shadow.

Admittedly, the times when we have a special friend or a group of friends are often the happiest and most secure; but, as scrutiny will show, they are often periods marked by stagnation or regression.

Each individual deserves honor and recognition, not just from a teacher whose job it is to encourage each student, but from his or her peers. To honor everyone promises significant conscious learning and a significant boost of one's confidence and self-respect. Respect for those who are different from ourself is the hallmark of the inner integration of ego and shadow. Toni and I believe that particular people are in our lives for a vital reason, to teach us by reflecting our nature back to us. When we accept each individual as they are, they increase our knowledge of ourselves and others, and they increase our capacity to live directly through our heart. It is a path toward compassion for self and others. When a school—parents, teachers, students—strives to include and embrace everyone, that school becomes a haven for accelerated learning and growth. Inclusion is the ideal we sought and never reached. There are many forces involved in group education, however, that inhibit growth and self-knowledge, especially the need to conform to the expectations of society where competition and winning are the ideal.

Often a parent anxiously seeks a special friend for her child and orchestrates the formation of an exclusive relationship for her. But for us, children without best friends have a great advantage: They are free to turn inward and develop self-reliance, self-love, self-direction, and, above all, they remain free to love everyone.

Difficult relationships confront us head-on and provide an opportunity for growth. Abrasive siblings learn from each other, even in the heat of disagreement. Or should we trade children from family to family until nobody has to learn to deal with uncomfortable confrontations or boring incompatibilities?

It is important to notice a certain craziness in our society. An adult in America has almost total power to cut off anyone who causes him discomfort or who challenges him, criticizes him, or holds him accountable. Our adult society permits us to ignore or abuse anybody who does not flatter us. We are free to end a relationship with anyone who holds us responsible for our actions.

The vow of marriage voids our right to dishonor one particular individual. The birth of our children implies treasuring and honoring them as well. Yet, how difficult it is to fulfill one's responsibilities to just a few! Should we, therefore, avoid our obligations to the many?

From a spiritual point of view we owe the same respect, if not the same attention, to all people in our life. Taking responsibility for one's self means learning to be conscious of how one impacts everyone, all life, and the earth itself. For children to be held to that same standard may appear harsh to adults who themselves ignore it. But for us, respect and honor for all is the only viable path to self-love, self-esteem, and self-development, the only viable path to save the earth and the people on it from annihilation. It is, for us, therefore, irresponsible to not teach children how to honor all. Namaste!

Human life, if devoid of honor, often follows a repetitive pattern that leads to numbness instead of vitality, exploration, and authentic experience. This path that leads to comfort requires the minimum of effort. Little new thinking occurs, just the repetition of the same thoughts ad infinitum. Very cushy. One is satisfied to rehash endless variations of what one already knows. This old dance of life resembles sleepwalking, sure and customary as an old hat that fits exactly on the head and warms the heart with its old smell and familiar shape. In this trance one may ignore others like ships passing in the night and pretend to have no connection with those who are not one's special friends.

The raising of consciousness requires facing new challenges, foreign thoughts, and uncomfortable insecurities. It is only in dealing with the unknown that we come face to face with the mystery of our own life.

The unfamiliar is, at worst, discomforting and awkward, demanding new energy and active involvement. The unconscious groove is gone; everything seems unpredictable and spontaneous, requiring daring, prowess, and spunk. In this scenario, there are no roads or tracks to follow. Each forward step brings a new awareness, new fears, new choices, and, if one perseveres, a great awareness of the power of one's being.

All of life's challenges present the same choice: advance with faith in one's inner strength, or retreat in fear into the comfort of habit and accepted belief. From our point of view, teachers have a spiritual obligation to support the individual to take risks, to experience new friendships, and to consider alternative ideas. Trusting in one's own experience leads to faith in self *and* faith in the universe to meet one's spiritual needs. Education, as I understand it, leads the individual to confront his own fear, doubt, shame, and limitation in order to experience the greater power and brilliance of self.

A Choice

We have a choice to make in education. Either we use education to make kids obedient to conventional thinking, or we train them to think for themselves. Either we convince children that what others think about them should determine their actions, or we teach them that other's opinions are irrelevant to their individual choice. We continue to train kids to fit into society, or we dare them to lead the way and inspire them with the world's great stories. Either we implant in their psyches the idea that they are to learn what educational managers decide is best for them, or we implant the idea that they are to think for themselves and take responsibility for their own education and their own life. We train them to conform to the norm or we help open the door to a life of spiritual freedom.

A century and a half ago, corporations already made that choice for most of us by setting up "free" mandatory public schools. [See Book Two for details] Today, within that setting, only the strongest are able to resist the siren's call to conform to the world in order to earn a decent living. Only the strongest are able to resist their peers' anti-intellectual, anti-spiritual message to be cool—a message that creates angry conformity, emotional numbness, negativity, and violence. As a result, many students have been reduced to expressing their nature primarily through their clothes, their hair, or their tatoos.

I admit that many private schools have their own glamour to offer: Train to be one of the elite of the corporate world, a moral and model citizen of the new world order. Be the cream of the crop. Learn how to network with powerful people and to blur the distinction of ethical and unethical behavior while becoming a superstar in the business world. Learn the manners and ways of the rich so you will fit into elite society. I refer to the financial and social advantages provided by elite schools as "glamour," because they fail to address the basic needs of the individual: to become connected to one's deepest nature through creativity, inspiration, devotion, truth, beauty, inclusion, and integrity. The elite may need such grounding as well.

Or one can be trained to be a model Christian, with the correct beliefs to satisfy a particular sect. Learn the art of literal interpretation of the scriptures so that God will reward you, and those like you, with paradise. Learn to defend orthodoxy against radicals, socialists, and devils in sheep's clothing; learn to suspend critical thinking. This may help one to become an official Christian, confident in one's correct belief system, but one is not free to move on to the universal, symbolic level of understanding, and one cannot entertain inner guidance which conflicts with outer, prescriptive teaching.

Our freedom and our ability to think for ourselves are what once produced several generations of largely self-educated, self-reliant, independent, optimistic, and brilliant entrepreneurs: thinkers, farmers, and frontiersmen, men like John Adams, who were willing to be "abrasive" to remain loyal to their principles. Our current times cry out for spiritually attuned individuals who are able to read, to think, while following a reliable internal guide that is in touch with the spiritual world.

There is a choice to be made between school books and real books, between texts and primary sources, between Dick, Jane, Spot and their successors or genuine fairy tales and mythology from around the world. We can choose between tomes composed of bits of literature or selections such as Homer's *Iliad* and *Odyssey*, the Greek plays, Pythagorus' teaching, stories of the Buddha, stories of the Hopi and Sioux tribes and the examples of men like Ghandi and Martin Luther King who individualized the universal principles they lived by. Many novel-

118

ists preserve the same tradition, including: C.S. Lewis (*The Chronicles of Narnia, Out of the Silent Planet, Till We have Faces*), Lloyd Alexander (*The Black Cauldron, Tara Wanderer, The High King*), Susan Cooper (*Over Sea, Under Stone; The Dark is Rising; Greenwich; The Grey King; Silver on the Tree*) Mark Twain (*The Adventures of Tom Sawyer, The Adventures of Huckleberry Finn, A Connecticut Yankee in King Arthur's Court, The Prince and the Pauper*), E. L. Konigsberg (*From the Mixed-Up Files of Mrs. Basil E. Frankweiler, A Proud Taste of Scarlet and Miniver, The Second Mrs. Giaconda*), George MacDonald (*The Princess and the Goblin, The Princess and the Curdie, At the Back of the North Wind*), Madeline D'Engle (*A Wrinkle in Time, A Wind at the Door, A Swiftly Tilting Planet*), Mary Renault (*The King Must Die, Bull From the Sea, The Mask of Apollo, Fire From Heaven, The Praise Singer, The Persian Boy, Last of the Wine, Funeral Games*), J.R.R. Tolkien (*The Hobbit, The Lord of the Rings*), Kenneth Roberts' *Oliver Wiswell* and *Northwest Passage*.

A curriculum which includes a good deal of material from perennial thinking helps kids preserve their natural spirituality, their connection to earth and sky, to creativity, to the art of the great traditions. It supports their belief in their own goodness and intelligence and in the brotherhood and sisterhood of the great family of mankind. It is a tradition of thought which heals, embraces, inspires, and honors children as people who possess the innocence to carry the flame of spirit.

Inside every child there lives multiple potentials and great humanity. But kids educated in factories cannot fathom what lies within their being. Even kids with a great self-image have little inkling of the powers they possess and the voice that yearns to speak. Nevertheless, within all children lies a radiance and glory, a perfection of heart and being that I find totally inspiring. They are unconscious of the energy they exude and how it affects others. And unconscious, too, of their potential authority and the power of their word.

That power and dynamism that we ascribe to the historical Buddha and Jesus, to Gandhi, Lao Tzu, Chuang Tzu, Rumi, Krishna, William Blake, Tolstoy,

If we believe other people's percepitons instead of our own, we've disowned ourselves, and pretty soon we've stopped loving ourselves too. But if we value our perceptions and follow them, we can eventually be whole.

Arnold Mindel

Madame Blavatski, Harriet Tubman, George Washington, Martin Luther King, lives or sleeps, at each moment of our lives, in us. Each person has an ability to drastically influence others. That's exactly what these great men taught and manifested in their lives: All men, not the chosen few, are divine in nature. Those who believe otherwise give away their power and see only their own sins, their own limits, their own impotence. Their belief in their own littleness has been taught to them by people who were similarly diminished by their elders. The six thousand year tradition (and probably longer) of controlling others through fear and emotional blackmail (for their own benefit, of course), blinds one to one's own inherent powers of goodness and authority.

The perennial tradition which cherishes each individual's ability to communicate directly with the divine has always stressed treating others with dignity. Throughout several millennium it is that tradition which has fought against the great excesses of religious witch hunts and racial persecution. It was a belief in the perennial tradition that spurred Quakers and others to support the end of slavery and to provide the underground railroad to deliver as many as possible from the horrors of slave life. The perennial tradition needs to be revived and applied to the master/slave mentality in American schools. We will discuss this further in Book Three.

How could a man live at all if he did not grant absolution every night to himself and all his fellows.
Goethe

Switching from Isolation to Inclusion

For us, for The Well, Inclusion is the key to defining our culture. If one plays the game of better than or worse than others, more valuable or worthless, more deserving or less, more entitled or subservient, more intelligent or retarded, coded and not coded, one becomes isolated in a world of division. But if, and only if, one honors both self and others, an amazing switch occurs, a new reality pops up. It is much like the experience of switching channels on a television; one is abruptly whisked from Arnold Schwarzenegger in Terminator 2 to Julie Andrews singing "The Sound of Music," or to Peter Jennings reporting from Israel. With television, one switches effortlessly and instantaneously from one reality to another and adjusts to the change in seconds. In real life people are also capable of switching, if they are not punished or humiliated for doing so, if they possess flexibility.

Everyone experiences the shift which occurs in dreaming. Within a single dream one may be taken from a Mahler symphony to a pigmy elephant hunt in a flash. One may be eating oatmeal in one's very familiar kitchen and be suddenly conversing with a talking statue of Caesar. Of course, one might experience this dramatic alteration of consciousness under the influence of mescalin as well. The point is that switching need not involve a slow, laborious change over a long period of years, but it may occur as a sudden transformation which baffles the mind that is searching for a constant framework. The same suddenness of switching which is possible when choosing a station on television can happen within an individual. It can happen to people who do not take themselves too seriously, such as kids who still possess spontaneity and flexibility or adults who choose to change because they are sick of being stuck in their own morbidity.

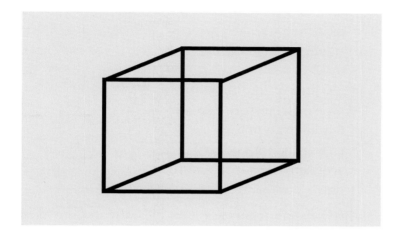

The switch in individuals is from one way of perceiving to another or from one attitude to another. Staring at the cube above, one can see it from a certain perspective, and then, suddenly, from another. One's first perception, so definite and obvious, changes to another which, moments before, would have been inconceivable.

In a similar way, one may be certain that another person is dead wrong and completely unreasonable. Then, by the power of grace, we are able to step into that person's shoes; suddenly, we are able to see the validity of her ideas or attitudes. Perhaps, the more certain we are that we are correct, the more certain it is that there is another way of looking at something.

This switch is well expressed in the dichotomies organized by David R. Hawkins in his brilliant book, *Power vs. Force: The Hidden Dominance of Human Behavior*. Hawkins describes the polarity encountered on moving from a life based on survival and force to a life based on one's inner power. When an individual relies on their own inner power, the following transformations occur:

- jealousy switches to admiration
- obligation turns into choosing
- indulgence into consideration
- unawareness into consciousness
- meddling into helpfulness
- rigidity into flexibility
- recklessness into courage
- resentment into forgiving
- pleasure transforms to joy
- flattery into praise
- enervation into nourishment
- acquisitiveness into gratitude
- doing into being

The ability to shift requires a level of awareness. First one must appreciate that one is free to choose how to respond to the variety of life experiences:

- triumph or defeat
- accomplishment or failure
- fortune or misfortune
- connection or separation
- success or disappointment
- love or fear
- peace or anxiety
- gain or loss

One must learn that each variation of response has its own consequence. For example, if one receives recognition in the form of a compliment, one might rebuff the compliment: "Oh, that was nothing," or "It's really no big deal." One might accept the compliment politely: "Thank you." Or one might allow that compliment to enter deeply into one's heart: "That means a lot to me." Each way of responding subtlely changes our future experience.

Or if one experiences disappointment, one might counter with "She hates me," or "I knew I would be rejected," or "I'll never do that again." On the other hand, one's response might be "Well, I'm glad I tried," or "Perhaps it wasn't meant to be," or "Next time I'll be prepared." Each person has the power to decide whether to be defeated by disappointment or whether to use such experience for motivation, for learning.

> Not in the clamour of the crowded street,
>   Not in the shouts and plaudits of the throng,
> But in ourselves are triumph and defeat.
> **Henry Wadsworth Longfellow**

Those who are spiritually healthy and have positive self-esteem possess the flexibility to weigh their reactions and make choices which further their goals. But those who are mired in self-pity react automatically. They must first

> The mind is its own palace, and in itself
> Can make a heaven of hell, a hell of heaven.
> **John Milton**

work to overcome a negative self-image. Our students, Henry and Alice, thought they were stupid, constantly comparing themselves to brilliant George and Freda. Henry tended to be sullen and quiet and often claimed to be bored; Alice seemed to have little ability to concentrate although she missed nothing in terms of the relationships of her friends. Special tutoring sessions for both children met with some success, but it did not change their view of themselves.

But when Henry's teacher regularly pointed out to him examples of his unusual ability to compute mentally, his skill in writing articulate poems, and his keen sense of observation in science, Henry shifted, emotionally and intellectually. When she said, "That poem is amazingly descriptive and brilliant. Would you be willing to read it out loud to the rest of the class?" something inside Henry clicked to the on position. He wanted to read it. The enthusiastic response of his classmates also helped him to see all kinds of new possibilities.

Henry was no longer inaccessible and sullen. He brightened when he was invited to play. He took pride in explaining a math solution and served as an example for others who were less advanced in math. He began science projects at home and reported on them in class. He became responsive and alert and saw the positive qualities in others. He was motivated to consider the possibilities in his life. He had learned the art of switching. Now, when he was stuck, he could switch by himself.

Alice, on the other hand, felt like a general failure at school but brightened when given responsibility in a non-academic area. Her teacher asked her to set up and supervise a few soccer practices for younger children. Her challenge was to create an atmosphere where the kids felt successful executing a few simple soccer drills. Alice turned out to be a master at seeing the potential in others and in communicating to them how competent they were. And by giving to others what she was unable to give directly to herself, she, with the help of her teacher's input, duly accepted her success. As it turned out, she was a natural teacher who understood how desperately her students needed encouragement.

Nothing significant was done to help her with her work, but she had suddenly become motivated to do well and ignored her record of failure. When she saw her own performance improve, she was able to see that by changing her attitude on the spot she could be successful.

> Our doubts are traitors, and make us lose
> The good we oft might win, by fearing to attempt.
> **William Shakespeare**

Tracy and David also were convinced that they were losers at school. Tracy had lived in the deep shadow of a brother whom her father had long considered a mathmatical genius, deserving of every opportunity for advanced math instruction. She considered herself stupid. Yet Tracy, who was extremely compassionate, gained confidence while taking care of the horses, goats, and llamas in the barn where she had a daily job cleaning the stalls and feeding the animals. Although she was too young to be a supervisor, she wrote to me one summer and included a list of reasons why, despite her age and her grade level, she was uniquely qualified for the job.

Later, true to her word, as a young barn supervisor, she excelled not only in handling the animals, but also in training and organizing the three older children who worked under her command. Her brother had no time for the barn.

Tracy's other passion was singing. She excelled in chorus and sang many solos and duets in musicals. Tracy gave outstanding performances in a variety of musical productions, and she became a commanding lead performer in musicals. As a result, her academics soared, and she realized that her talents were not limited to taking care of animals and music. She became very confident and no longer felt the need to compete with her brother for recognition. She knew, however, that she was smart, and she proved it again when she attended boarding school.

David did everything he could to avoid academic work. He hated to be in class and was especially resistant to expose himself through writing. Without the strong parental support from a father who had experienced similar difficulties, David would have given up. David was like Tracy in many ways; his love of animals led him to become barn supervisor for several years after Tracy graduated. But, unlike Tracy, he disliked singing. His forte was helping with all manner of physical work: snow blowing and shovelling during snow storms (he had a knack for repairing broken machines); mowing grass; building fences, sheds, or theater sets; making props; hanging and setting lighting; running the lighting board; stacking wood and carting heavy objects all over campus; as well as serving as general handy-man for a number of teachers. Much of his confidence came from his father who allowed him to drive a car or truck on private land, and to run a backhoe and test the water table under his direction. David knew he was an exceptional, responsible worker even by adult standards.

I allowed David to miss hundreds of hours of regular class time to work on projects which benefitted the school, because, in my view, there is nothing that builds genuine self-esteem like doing what one loves to do while taking responsibility on one's own to do an excellent job. Whatever David undertook, he did well.

David's resistance to classroom work never completely disappeared, but his brilliance in academics steadily developed. He enlivened classrooms because he was an independent thinker who was not afraid to present his opinions to others. He learned to pay attention to details while reading in many fields and kept us all on our toes. He won respect among his peers not only for his practical skills, but also for his intellect.

Each of these four children represent examples of change over time. Often, however, when children came to the Well from a school where they had experienced failure, the change was more immediate and required little or no special intercession by adults. The fresh start, coupled with a supportive environment available in a new school, made possible what before had seemed impossible. The changes that occurred in these students illustrate how once someone has developed generalized positive self-esteem, he or she can move from the mundane to the divine in a twinkling.

Do we not all, consciously or unconsciously, align ourselves with different forms of energy, such as the energy associated with a thirst for revenge or the peace made possible by forgiveness? To be connected with others, with the universe as a whole, is to align ourselves with inclusiveness, with love. The greatest choice of all, in my opinion, is the decision as to which energies we wish to be controlled by. In my experience we are not the rulers of anything, but we are, inevitably, ruled by a combination of productive or destructive energies. What we consciously choose to do, repeatedly, over time, strongly influences what rules us.

It is not enough to make a mental choice; one must actively practice that choice in one's life before it changes consciousness. If our thoughts and actions are not in agreement, or if our thoughts and feelings collide, hypocrisy results. Hypocrisy siphons away our power to the never-never land of spiritual paralysis. Hypocrisy splits our will and alienates us from our self and others.

The energies of Love and Hatred, one aligned with inclusion, one with manipula-

A Dream

In my dream I am abandoned, deserted,
Forsaken by my wife, my beloved,
All prospects dashed, all loss secured.
I feel nauseous, broken, lost, bewildered,
Anxious to the bones of my being.

How can all power be forfeit in a moment?
How can all meaning have no meaning now?
What power owns my power?
What fact destroyed all assumptions?

In this fantasy I find all disillusionment contained:
All my fears trace back into my infancy,
All self-doubts, all negativity, all inflexibility.
In this simple, unnerving scenario lies my ruin,
In this hell I strive to hate my whole life,
To rip by the roots all I have planted and nurtured,
To damn myself eternally; to forsake every shred of hope.

Then I think of spirit, my own spirit within:
Do I not live in an Invisible land, as the son of the living God?
Is not my inheritance His love, His beauty, His power?
Do I not still yearn to say, "The Father and I are One?"
Cannot miraculous God put Humpty Dumpty together again?

I yearn for a clear vision of my own goodness and perfection
As seen through God's eyes,
Then as seen through my eyes.
Can I not bring my nightmare within to my Father's realm
That it may yield a great blessing, a great harvest of fruit?
May I not now discern my strong roots
In Heaven and my graceful branches in Paradise?

Jay Garland

tion, are real. And the ideas derived from a loving heart nourish and enlarge us as those derived from hate diminish us. One who comes from Love says "Yes" to Life; then one invites the Self to participate fully in one's own path to self-discovery.

Plant blessings, and blessing will bloom;
Plant hate, and hate will grow;
You can sow today — tomorrow will bring
the blossom that proves what sort of thing
Is the seed — the seed you sow.

Sarah K. Bolton

Possibilities for the Future

The Well School was founded as a community which honored the principle of Inclusion. The more deeply we became involved in that community, the more clearly we saw the necessity of establishing heart-to-heart connections among all members in order to communicate truthfully, fully, and unambiguously.

We were often aware that in some sense, we were pioneers. In order to nourish and develop the sacred qualities of children, Toni and I needed to raise our level of consciousness and help others in the community—children, parents, and teachers—to raise theirs.

Central to the success of our mission was awareness of the multifaceted nature of children in general, and the special abilities of each child in particular. We knew that the core of an authentic curriculum was presenting choices to children, supporting their inner self, and helping them to integrate the emotional, mental, and spiritual aspects of human nature.

We recognized that much of who we are as individuals remains invisible unless we fearlessly express ourselves. We are not our hands and feet, for without them we would still exist. We are not our hair and skin; if we lost them we would remain. We are in our essence, mind and soul and spirit, elusive stuff, but very powerful. One must be, however, connetced to one's power in order to use it. Power rests

Invisible Dew

*The invisible dew is airy
And brings no sudden chill.
It penetrates the skin and bones
To execute its will.*

*And everywhere it wanders
It devours a little space,
So lighter I am fashioned,
More porous through its grace.*
Jay Garland

principally in the invisible world, the creative world as potential. Inasmuch as one is overly impressed by the visible, in fact, one loses one's creative power.

The external world is itself the manifestation of the creative, invisible world. The law of cause and effect states that what is clearly and definitively held by mind and spirit automatically manifests in the visible world. There are no exceptions. One's life, therefore, displays the nature of one's beliefs, whether those beliefs be limiting or unlimiting, conflicting or aligned.

While objective reality represents the visible effects of invisible causes, according to the law of creative thought, it has been seen by materialists as the whole of reality. Scientists (the priesthood of our society) are really of two minds, those who accept the role of consciousness in the creative process of a spiritual universe and those who claim that mind and spirit have no effect on the mechanical laws of the universe. The first group finds meaning in subjective, inner experience, and, therefore, meaning in life. The second declares that subjective experience is a fantasy which is divorced from reality. Among the first group, some have acknowledged the importance of subjective experience as a formative factor in the universe. The newer perception of separate, but linked, objective and subjective realities seems to be yielding to a broader single system, slowly being knitted together as one unity.

The principles of science are as invisible as those of spirit. We never see atomic structure, gravity or electricity, but we come to accept them as real. The principles of electricity explain the nature of light, heat, or motive power. Even the mathematics on which science ultimately depends is invisible. When we turn on a light we don't see the amperage, the wattage, the voltage, or the equation which relates these abstractions. We experience only the light.

The science which mathematically relates the invisible causes through equations or laws is part of the same branch of science which deals with the impersonal, unbending laws of the inevitable manifestation of what is known. Science, even true spiritual science, is no respecter of privilege

Heart

Heart is the pleasure
to which we aspire

Heart is the treasure,
the doorway to fire

Heart is the tower
to climb to the skies

Heart is the power
to speak through the eyes

Heart is the reason
to enter within

Heart is the lesion
where pain has been

Heart is the ocean
that dances with light

Heart is the sun
the hawks who take flight

Heart is the artist
That Colors the Night

Heart is the singer
That voices delight

Heart is the fountain,
The power to make whole

Heart is the laughter
The voice the soul

Heart is the dancer
That glides through our
woes.

Heart is the seeker
Which sniffs out the rose.

Jay Garland

or earthly power. Prayers for special privilege contradict the universality of the spiritual law which plays no favorites.

What has been created by the mind—lack, disease, unhappiness—can be undone by the mind, if one is willing to alter one's beliefs and loyalties, that is, if one makes heart and mind congruent. This happens when mind surrenders to spirit and accepts the heart as the commander-and-chief. Mind, as servant to spirit, ceases to confuse, because its chief function is clarity, organization, and analysis.

Since all happens according to invariable laws or principles, the pursuit of health, abundance, and happiness follows directly from one's mental and spiritual assumptions. In my opinion, an enlightened approach combines a trust in the individual experience of truth with action which is in accordance with spiritual principles.

Since all causes are invisible, whether they are scientific or spiritual causes, all power, intelligence, and purpose lie in the invisible realm, the realm of mind and spirit. Those who look to the invisible world of causes, whether they be scientists, economists, healers, or candlestick makers, all who are creative in any sense, deal with the invisible principles of the transformation of energy.

In the subjective realm the invisible rules all things through the universal heart (spirit connection). Breath (spirit) is the doorway to the invisible. Heart and breath work together as regulators, determining the degree of consciousness and, therefore, the accessibility to wisdom. Together they either open or shut the entrance to various levels of reality.

Moving into deeper levels of consciousness requires intuitively using the heart (love principle) to screen every experience. The heart is a trustworthy guide to determine the quality of each encounter. It takes the temperature of every situation, diagnosing, and sensing; it interprets signs. The heart factors in what lies behind the scenes, including the most subtle nuances; it reads intent and double intent and purpose. It recognizes significance. The heart, therefore, is a grand interpreter and not just a receiver. How does it do this? How does it perceive so many levels simultaneously? The heart is attuned to different levels of reality, so it picks up a wide variety of vibrations. It reads what minds and hearts and bodies are broadcasting. It is only when one's radio or television is tuned to a particular station that the music or speech is intelligible. But the heart picks up many frequencies at once; rather than tune in and focus on one, it does the reverse—it listens to the total projection as a whole and then processes it. It scans the entire field. Here we see the extraordinary intelligence of the heart as a multifunctional receiver and as an interpreter of data. But more amazing is that the heart is incapable of misreading. It is a totally accurate instrument which delivers both instantaneous apprehension and a delayed sifting and re-sifting while searching for significance and purpose. Because the individual heart is tied to the universal heart, it uses its own knowledge as well as the resources of the central information bank, the universal mind.

Using heart as one's primary antennae implies making heart the primary focus of attention. In listening to others, if heart and mind are equally dominant, great confusion and misinformation result because one simultaneously reads the conflicting messages of both. Then there is no clear center of authority. Gaining consciousness of clear heart messages is neither simple or easy. It requires a quiet mind and an strong intent. It involves discipline that is gained through regular attunement to spirit and by leading a simple, unfettered life.

As one learns to respond to messages of the heart, one reads ever more complex messages and adapts to the increased range of information which is received. Since the heart must open in stages over the course of many years (or even over the course of a lifetime) one is at first like a baby learning to walk, trying to integrate and sift through all the information from the environment and from the nervous system. At ever deeper levels, the heart has direct and immediate connection to the divine.

It is time for educators to approach their work through the universal heart, not to reduce the potential of human nature to serve the powers that be, but to serve the transformation of human potential into luminous, creative individual expression of what lies beneath.

Our attempt to create a heart-based education at The Well was also an indirect attempt to bring joy and life into the educational process. Our next book in *The Challenges of Authentic Education* series details the important role that raising consciousness has in authentic education and gives examples of activities which specifically served that purpose. Our commitment to make love the energy and fuel of The Well originated from our experiences in Eskimo communities and was strengthened through our experiences at The Well. To us, authentic education opens the door to joy and love, the lifeblood of experience, because joy and love connect directly with the mystery called Life.

We have learned during our time at The Well that Self is the source of life, health, wisdom, creativity, and joy. To know oneself as a treasure is to realize the full capacity of one's inner being. To know others as part of the same treasure exponentially broadens the vision.

Education can be part of the process of allowing children to open to possibility, for children are, indeed, the promise of humanity. "Be ye as little children," reminds us to recapture the lost potential to be One with Life in consciousness. Clean air, though invisible, without taste or odor, meets the requirements of matter. Love, joy, and interior light meet the requirements of Spirit; they open the door to mental health, to beauty, to peace, to genius, to possibility.

Meditation which focuses attention, not to breathing in the visible air, but to inhaling the abundant Love of the universe transforms consciousness. Not a small step, but a great leap to take, for regularly breathing love leads directly to the consciousness of the omnipresence of spirit. Bringing focus to the invisible leads to the spiritual realm where all is possible. Maintaining focus is the key to crossing the ocean of consciousness to enter the expanded consciousness of the universal, the original home of every child.

This brings us to the question of inheritance. Inheritance, according to traditional thinking, confers

Holy, Holy, Holy

Holy, holy, holy are the eyes of love;
They speak of the luminous light
That informs this dark, dark night.

Fire, fire, fire is the heart of love.
A torch, a beacon of the living light
That awakes the dead to flight.

Tender, tender, tender is the breath
Of sleeping child with loving light.
Here lies the door to the Infinite.

Oh, Oh, Oh - eyes, heart, breath
The instruments of mercy mild.
Let's all sing of the Infinite.

Jay Garland

authority and wealth and separates those with a noble blood line from the rest. But the oneness of Spirit (if you prefer, God) guarantees the nobility of all children because inheritance defines one's entitlements. Being a child of Spirit confers the blessings of Spirit, its unrestricted love, its qualities, its gifts. Inheritance, in so many ways, defines ones being, and since what one is in nature cannot be added to, but only revealed, it defines one's potential as well.

To accept the child, in all his glory and potential, is the first step to transform the nature of education. It is also the abiding principle of everything that follows. The principle of Inclusion is the basis of a community which helps to protect and nourish the divine being of each child.

Look Outward, Look Inward

Look Outward,
Magnify Mind!
Live in time.
Limit being,
Limit wealth,
Limit experience,
Limit love.

Look Inward!
Magnify Spirit!
Live in Eternity & Now!
Multiply Being & Power!
Find Abundance beyond Desire!
Ride on the wings of Experience!
Love of the Heart creates All!

Jay Garland

Toni, Kambrah and Ak in Pilot Station, Alaska

Toni and Jay in college, 1959

Maggie Tallo, Kambrah, Toni and Ak, Pilot Station

Martina Heckman, Jay and Toni, Pilot Station

136

Brick House cellar after cleaning

Jay and Toni in June of 1968

First look at location for new school (with dead elms), 1967

Ak at age 3 with Camel (only 3 months old) and Bob Tail

Jay, Kambrah and Toni

Jay teaching "upper school" in 1967 (Wendy, Jim, Packy, Jo, Mary B.)

138

Recess at The Well (Dan, Jeff M., Tara, Bonnie), Spring of 1968

Wendy riding Jenny with Jay, Dan, Matt and Ann

Tara with classmates at Whit's Ski Tow

Kambrah's first poetry recital at the Eldredge
Barn, 1967

"A Midsummers Night Dream" at the Eldredge Barn

"Green Pastures" at the Eldredge Barn

Recess at The Well, Spring of 1968

"Oma" - Ursula Garland

Raphy and Roger

Haying in New Ipswich, NH (Raphy, Cindy and Danda)

Sarah B. with others Playing
"Eskimo Baseball"

Contradancing

"The Well Ensemble" at Coffee House (Marybeth, Nate, Jo, Erica, Caleb

Kate and Kambrah at Coffee House

A typical gathering at the Garland's dining room table

Toni and Jay at Cindy's wedding

Toni

The Well and Family

Grace:
For Health and Strength and Daily Bread
We give Thee Thanks, O Lord

Grace:
We thank thee for our daily bread.
For blessings on our table spread
Our Father in heaven.

Before I begin my saga of our family and The Well, I want to say, that though Jay and I have pretty much always been a team and that we have schooled together since we were twelve and taught together since we were twenty, Jay is the educator. It is even expressed in our physical vision. I'm near-sighted; he's far sighted. I often see the "up close and personal;" he gets the more distant and more comprehensive picture. For the most part, it has been and is a good combination; occasionally it gets a little sticky. A true educator must have a vision, and Jay has provided that for us all. He saw clearly that there was genius in every child. The intention to provide avenues which would allow that genius to be expressed became one of our major missions. In many cases, we did a pretty good job. In some cases we failed, but the genius still existed.

My hope is in some way to convey the luck and inspiration that we have enjoyed as a couple, as a family, and as a school. We first became acquainted when we were twelve years old, entering the seventh grade in Mount Vernon, New York, a suburb next to New York City. I had just barely descended from the trees, having been an incorrigible tom-boy up until then. Until the seventh grade, kindergarten had been my only good year in school. That was the one and only year in my early school career that involved actually doing things in school. Grades

To wonder at beauty,
Stand guard over truth
Look up to the noble
Look up to the good
Leads man on his journey
To right in his thinking
To right in his duty
To light in his thought.
Rudolf Steiner

The ultimate lesson all of us have to learn is unconditional love, which includes not only others but ourselves as well
Elizabeth Kubler-Ross

one through six involved reading, writing, and sitting, none of which caught my imagination.

Three schools consolidated at the junior high level in our school district, so there were many new faces that first fall day of seventh grade. One of those new faces belonged to Jay, who sat in front of me in our home room and next to me or behind me in all other classes, except gym. On that first day of school, I had no idea that he was so handsome; his face bore a surface of huge scabs and sores caused by a horrendous, over- the- handlebars bike accident. Nonetheless, my interest in school picked up immediately.

Jay was the first boy that I felt attracted to and that I hadn't evaluated on the basis of his athletic ability, though he was a good athlete. He made my heart pound, try as I would to pretend to act otherwise.

I don't think I missed more than a handful of school days in those three years of junior high school, which was notable, since I barely made a regular school appearance in the first six years. We sat near each other in class, annoying or distracting each other, getting assignments, or chatting.

It wasn't until June of our ninth-grade-year that we went on our first official date. We had seen plenty of each other in and out of school, but going to Jones Beach on Long Island, New York, marked our first official date. Double dating with Jay's older brother meant we had a driver to take us to the beach. Both of us, incredibly shy and awkward with each other, kept conversation to a minimum. Suddenly, the punching, teasing, joking, and laughing of the preceding years vanished. Generally hyperactive and very athletic, I found I could hardly move when we got to the beach. Usually I had an opinion about everything when asked what I'd like to do, but that day I could only reply, "I don't care." We did finally go into the freezing cold ocean. We rode the waves, splashed each other hilariously, got caught broadside by errant waves, and ducked under them, only to come up and do it all over

The Eternal Three

There are two men in the world, who
Are crossing my path I see,
And one is the man I love,
The other's in love with me.

And one exists in nightly dreams
Of my somber soul evermore,
The other stands at the door of my heart
But I will not open the door.

And one once gave me a vernal breath
Of happiness squandered—alack!
The other gave me his whole, long life
And never got an hour back.

And one lives hot in the song of my blood
Where love is pure, unbound—
The other is one with the humdrum day
Where all our dreams are drown.

Between these two every woman stands,
In love, beloved, and white—
And once every hundred years it happens
That both in one unite.

Tove Ditlevsen

again. When we left the water, exhausted, we returned to our place on the beach and flopped down on our towels side by side. Jay shyly put his arm across my back and shoulder. Thrilled, I couldn't move and lay there like a statue. There we stayed for the next two hours, too shy to disengage, too thrilled to change position, too socially inept to know what to do next. Neither of us spoke. Finally, Roger rescued us by saying, "Time to go."

"Gosh, you guys are red!" Roger's date said. "Let's see your back, Toni. You probably have a white patch where Jay's arm was."

Oh my god, I thought. My mother will see it! What will she think? I was sure this would be unacceptable. Guilt and embarrassment burned within me, compounding the heat from the sun. What a little thing it is now; what a huge moment it was then. What humor there is now; what seriousness there was then. To my relief, no white telltale signs appeared, only total redness from my first early summer exposure to the sun. In those days, no one used sun block. If we used anything, it was baby oil to increase the intensity of the rays. Jay, too, glowed. We rode home, silently, sitting close to each other in the back seat of the car, Jay's arm, once again draped awkwardly over my shoulder, once again completely uncomfortable and once again, utterly in heaven.

Later that evening, when the sunburn showed its true degree, one side of me, the back side, glowed a brilliant cadmium red, the front side, just pink. I could barely move, but I took great solace in believing I had been on the perfect date. By morning, my skin had practically returned to normal, and in a couple of days, the red had turned to brown or formed freckles, depending on the location on my body.

A week went by and I hadn't heard from Jay. My belief in the perfect date began to waver. Two weeks went by, and I still hadn't heard from him. Crushed, I went to Michigan with my family for our summer vacation in a small town where my grandmother lived. Oh, my gosh, how overjoyed I was to get a letter from Jay. The remembrance is a fond recollection of the fragrance of the oiled post office floors, the squeak of the wood as I made my way to my grandma's post office box, and the thrill of spying a letter through the little, glass, mailbox door.

Jay's letter described the aftermath of our beach date. It turned out that because his skin was fairer than mine, his Jones Beach sunburn registered third degree burns. Yikes! This had put him out of commission for quite a while. We corresponded a lot that summer. Fourteen-year-old bliss!

The thought of another date, catapulted me into ridding myself of my tomboy-calloused hands. I wanted to be prepared for hand holding, so I took my grandma's advice, and soaked my hands in lotion each night and wore an old pair of cotton dress gloves to bed. I can't remember if it did any good, but at least my attempt to be more feminine seemed to do the trick for confidence building. I found it very hard to give up my tomboy roots, and in fact, I was never really able to, but somehow, as time went on, those roots lost their importance to me.

Our contact waned in high school, though I was pretty aware of his whereabouts. One of Jay's "good" friends told me that Jay liked some one else. In that case, I thought, too bad for you. Pride can be so devastating to a relationship, I was to discover. Insulted and hurt, our friendship ended. Years later, I found out that Jay's friend had lied to me so that I would date him. There were a lot of life lessons in that series of events.

Our friendship revived in our senior year of high school. During the two year separation from each other, both of us had learned to talk on dates, as well as other things. My gosh, did Jay ever learn to talk, and it was interesting to me. He had questions and ideas about everything— the stars, family, plays he had read, freedom. In his mind freedom was a huge topic. He was the rebel without a cause. Dare to be yourself. My god, myself, I thought. Who am I? Dare to do what you want. I always thought I did do what I wanted. Of course, until Jay came along in our senior year, I had pretty much always done what was expected of me, so what I wanted was congruent with expectations. No problem.

Saturday nights, we often talked until early in the morning; I can still conjure up the smell of the leather seats in the old Ford convertible. I can even feel the strong upholstery thread that had unravelled from the car cushion as I wound and unwound it around my index finger, making my finger puff up and down as we talked, our feet propped on the dashboard, Jay's lanky arm around my shoulder.

Although freshman year of college sent us on our separate journeys, Jay to Massachusetts, and I to Michigan, Cupid did his job and brought us together permanently in March 1958, after a few futile attempts at eloping. We were married in Cambridge, the Spring of our sophomore year in college, in a church on Harvard Square, located at the end of Church Street. To this day, I have no idea what the name of the church was nor what denomination it represented. Actually, the only things I do remember about the ceremony are the feeling of our boney fingers, tightly interlaced while standing at the altar, and how badly the minister shook as he held the book he read from.

The excitement and joy of the early years of marriage spill into today when I recall the incredible feeling of love and power we had then. We knew we could accomplish anything we wanted. In fact, life was so great, every once in a while, I would worry when the other shoe would fall. It didn't. Even now, tempered with time and experience, I am fully aware those possibilities still exist, and can happen at a moment's notice. So, do I feel lucky? More lucky than can I say.

We taught for seven years, two in Alaska, two in Massachusetts, one in New Hampshire, and then two more in Alaska. We moved from Pilot Station, Alaska, a small Eskimo village on the Lower Yukon, to Peterborough, New Hampshire, in July of 1967, each twenty-seven years old, I with the five month edge on twenty-seven, with a daughter, Kambrah, five years old and a three -year- old son, Akhil.

Our children still harbor some strong feelings about their names. Take note, they were born in the '60s when we, as young adults and potential parents, felt freed of our traditions. Our intention was to

People who address you as buddy or pal are not being overly friendly- they've just forgotten your name.

dissolve boundaries; our hope was to expand or erase the existing limits. We felt that having boundaries meant you expended a lot of wasted energy in a defense system promoting exclusion. (Later our children's generation, worked hard to re-establish boundaries). We worked hard on those names, believing that the naming of children was crucial and deserved the utmost consideration. For us, the process of naming our children had great power. We felt that unusual names with strength and beauty would give our children a huge advantage. We hoped that it would remind us to encourage the beauty, strength, and wisdom of each of them. We never doubted that each child would have those attributes. We spent a lot of time arranging and re-arranging syllables to please the ear for the name of each unborn baby.

Of course, my father was not a youth in the sixties, so when he heard Ak's name, he said in no uncertain terms, "When that kid grows up, he's going to kick you right square in the ass." He was fairly prophetic, but the kick wasn't just for the naming. My dad added with some reluctance, "Well, at least when he goes into business, it will be a helluva asset! People will remember a name like that." Business meant a great deal to my father. Of course, the pseudonym Ak used in his first business making personalized song tapes for children was not Akhil, but *John*. Go figure!

We returned to New Hampshire in time for the haying season. With the annual New Ipswich Garland family haying done—a two to three week period devoted to watching the weather, cutting hay while the sun shone, and bringing it in to store for the winter. Ever since Jay and I were in college, hay time was always a blast. When we first cut the fields, it was just to clear back the rough brush that had been creeping in over the years before Jay's folks moved to the farm. Jay drove the tractor, and I rode on a mowing machine that consisted of a cutting bar, a huge metal seat, and a foot lever that controlled the height of the cutting bar. Jay gunned the motor whenever we came to challenging brush, the speed of the tractor controlling the speed of the teeth in the cutting bar, making them whiz faster. Whap! Down fell the brush as I fought to stay on the jolting and tipping metal seat, lowering and raising the cutting bar to avoid any rocks—New England pastures are riddled with rocks. We returned for lunch or dinner each day with missing "teeth," luckily only the ones on the mowing machine. Barley, Jay's father, patiently replaced the chipped or broken blades and sharpened the good ones for our next field adventure.

Over the next few years Barley and Ursula, Jay's parents, turned worn out soil into fertile, productive earth, growing lush green grass that made marvelous hay. Their secret was the neighboring farms' chicken houses that contained abundant amounts of chicken manure. Free for the taking. It wasn't exactly free, since it was incredibly hot and smelly work to procure the fertilizer. The manure was so deep and so close to the ceiling that Barley and Jay had to bend over to get inside the coops. Getting each pitchfork of manure dumped out the window without breathing the horrendous ammonia as it filled the air, struggling as the vapors stung their eyes and nearly blinded them, and finally, gasping for air at the open window, was a triumph. The cleaning of the chicken house was a Herculean feat.

When the New Ipswich farm began to really produce hay, some machinery was located and bought: a baler, a tedder machine, and a mower. The temperamental 1938 dump truck remained a part of the routine, lending a certain amount of tension to the haying process up until the fram was sold in the mid-'70s.

Haying was the highlight of the extended family gathering each summer. Seeing a good stretch of weather coming, Barley declared "Time to cut." The mowing began and the skies were watched intently as the grass fell beneath the cutting bar. Kids rode and drove the tractors as the grass was cut or windrowed. We all converged on the farm from our various homes. Initially it was just family that did the work, but later many friends came to New Ipswich to help with the haying. Hay wagons and the old dump truck were pitched high with bales. Mothers with babies rode the wagons and everyone sang, as we headed for the barn with a full load. Picking and throwing bales onto the wagons or into the old dump truck got us in great mental and physical condition for the summer. The truck sometimes dumped at the wrong time, causing some annoyance and a great deal of hilarity. That occurred at least once a season, a reminder to keep us all alert to the possibility. Once at three o'clock in the morning when the night air was hot, humid and hazy, with thunderstorms threatening, the fully loaded truck took an unrequested dump. Rain was imminent. One could smell it coming. I think that was the only time I ever heard Jay's Dad swear as we all scrambled to reload the bales. Barley had a real obsession about keeping every bale dry and making excellent hay. We did manage to get it all under the cover.

Each day, as the thermometer rose, Oma brought her brand of juice out into the field every few hours for a quick drink. Slop, she called it—a diluted concoction of lemonade, grape, and orange juice—which tasted like nectar from the gods and quenched the thirst like nothing else on earth.

One year, someone brought a homemade drink they had made from dandelion blossoms and honey, a concoction that was called switchel. It was very thin, effervescent, and had a pleasantly sour flavor. It was served ice cold. Late in the afternoon, out in the field, the brew went down our throats easily, and had a cooling and quenching effect as we hastily swallowed. It wasn't long, however, before we were all—kids and adults—spread out on the grass, totally relaxed, laughing, feeling the effects of the alcohol content which, of course, no one had realized until it was to late. We quit early that day, and we never again used switchel as a thirst quencher during the weeks of hay making.

As soon as the kids could reach the pedals, they drove the tractors since they were too small to lift the bales. At the end of each day, Oma always had a huge feast for everyone: German potato salad, piles of fresh vegetables, hamburgers or roast beef, incredibly green salads with a dressing I tried to make but never could, and of course strawberry short cake, or pounds of German pound cake, cookies, and enormous bowls of fresh fruit. The women did the dishes after dinner. Oma never had nor wanted a dishwasher. Washing dishes was a pleasure since it provided gossip-time and sanity checks on the part of the sisters-in-law. At these times, we discovered there were other traits attached to genes in the Garland males besides tongue chewing and uncommon height. As the commonality of characteristics in our husbands was discovered, gales of laughter followed. I think the love that the sisters-in-law had for each other and their husbands, as well as the humor that they shared was the real glue of the family.

Cousins played together outside until they could no longer see because of the dark. Oma offered them sparklers from her enormous stash. We oohed and aahed as each sparkler caught fire, sending forth pinpoints of random light in every direction. Each child's face lit up with awe and excitement as his hissing charge created large, glittering figure-eights in the night. Dancing around the yard with their sparklers the children looked like sequined fireflies. When the last one was spent and dutifully placed in a bucket of water, "just in case," the children came in and begged to spend the night upstairs. Of course, they were allowed to sleep over. We would be returning early the next morning anyway. "This way we will get more sleep," the children told us. Somehow, I wasn't sure that was true, but it was summertime. Upstairs they went with nary a peep. The grown-ups talked downstairs while the children talked and drifted off to sleep. Somehow, the day seemed perfect and incredibly blessed. Haying ended in 1974 when Barley died and the farm was sold. We felt very fortunate for the wonderful times we all had spent together and miserable that the fifteen years of haying had ended.

In July of 1967, we moved into a huge house on Middle Hancock Road in Peterborough, New Hampshire. Jay's parents, along with his brother and sister-in-law, Peter and Mary, had found the house for us when we were still living in Alaska. We had asked them to look for a large house that would accommodate both our family and the school, because we were sure that we couldn't afford two separate places, a home and a school building. Fortunately, they were able to find one

Begin

*This is now. Now is. Don't
postpone til then. Spend*

*spark of iron on stone.
Sit at the head of the table;*

*dip your spoon in the bowl.
Seat yourself next to your joy*

*and have your awakened soul
pour wine. Branches in the*

*spring wind, easy dance of
jasmine and cypress. Cloth*

*for green robes has been cut
from pure absence. You're*

*the tailor, settled among his
shop goods; quietly sewing.*

Jalalu'l-Din Rumi

which fit both requirements.

One hot July morning, five of us drove up the dirt driveway to a humongous brick structure built in 1906. Stuffed in our little green Volkswagon were our two children, Jay, Susie Green, a young Eskimo woman who had come with us from Alaska to help with our children and the starting of the school, and I. The red-orange bricks of the house had an unusual glazed luster and were said to have been shipped from Ireland, each one individually wrapped in straw. The house had not been lived in for five years, so it was no wonder it had an abandoned look. Huge, dead elms surrounded it and had spawned elm seedlings, growing out of all five chimneys.

Ak, then three, took a long hard look with his big sapphire-blue eyes and asked, "Mommy, where is Pilot Station from here?" I pointed to the northwest and answered, " Way through those woods and over the hills; it's quite a long way." It was clear that in his opinion this new place was no match for the one we had come from, but I guessed if he had an idea in which direction to head it would be all right. The explanation seemed to satisfy him. He was a real home-body, and the recent moving around had been disconcerting.

Every so often, the courses in the chimney bricks had wavy lifts from the thick elm roots, creating the impression that at any moment the chimneys might topple. Fortunately, each chimney, and there were five of them, was built like a fortress, with a tile flu encompassed by two thicknesses of rough bricks and finally faced with an outer layer of the glazed bricks. A heavy, granite capstone on each chimney also prevented them from falling. A dank and musty smell permeated the rooms, causing me to wonder if this could ever be a home.

It had never been completely finished. World War II had interrupted its completion for a while, and its enormous size slowed the finishing process and frustrated each new owner's attempt to complete it. Almost all the rooms had raw plaster and there were no baseboards or trim. Electric wires hung like spaghetti from the basement ceiling, dangling the old knob and tube wiring above the dirt floor. A huge bricked-in pool of water in the cellar was responsible for the musty, dank air that pervaded the house. Yet, the whole house, including the attic, had hardwood floors and beautifully plastered walls. Even the basement had sported plastered ceilings at one point, but over the years, the moisture had spoiled the earlier efforts of a plasterer, leaving large patches of uncovered lath, where the damp ceiling had succumbed to time and gravity.

That July, many Garlands, both adults and children, several other potential school families, and old college friends helped us clean, re-wire, and paint the huge house. It felt a little like refurbishing a battleship, knowing full well that when all the walls were finally painted, it would be time to start all over again.

Early one summer morning, Jay and his brother Roger, chainsaws in hand, ripped out the one grand feature of the house, a spectacular oak staircase that stood in the center of the building. Its position had kept one from freely going through the house from front to back. Jay's brother Peter, an architect, designed what he referred to as a ladder to replace the grand old staircase. Simple, yet beautiful in design, it took up half the width of the original staircase. The new staircase opened up the space, and provided direct access from one end of the house to the other by allowing room for a hallway. Beneath the ladder we built a stairway to the basement.

We painted and plastered morning, noon, and night. We removed wheelbarrow load after wheelbarrow load of dirt, bricks, and plaster from the basement, lowering and leveling the floor so we could put in drains, and later, a cement floor. Each time our friends came up from Boston or New York, they worked right along with us, fixing the house, readying the school, digging, plastering, and painting. Our friend Fred mentioned at the end of one such week-long stint that, if he didn't regain the use of his hands, he would never forgive us. Agony.

We consumed endless pots of spaghetti and bottles of imported wines. (Imported from Boston or New York by friends.) And blessedly, each Sunday, Ursula, provided a divine and delicious break from

Work in the invisible world at least as hard as you do in the visible.
Jalalu'l-Din Rumi

I have discovered the secret of happiness- it is to work, either with the hands or the head- something to do. It is the only safe and sure ground of happiness.
John Burroughs

the renovations—a roast beef Sunday dinner in New Ipswich, a neighboring village—for any and all Garlands. We all went home from those occasions with piles of leftovers, making meals a snap for the next few days. Looking back, the renovations went incredibly quickly, but at the time they seemed endless.

We held a "Tea" in August to present our educational ideas to interested neighbors and perspective parents. Mary Garland, Peter's wife, and mother of five of the incoming students, covered huge, gaping holes in the walls, created by unfinished doorways, with colorful Indian bedspreads. (These bedspreads were new, not yet the washed out, drab condition that our children took to college and referred to as "drug sheets.") Mary's masterful hand and eye transformed what just hours before had looked like a building imported from war-torn Europe into an orderly, artistic space, complete with refreshments. People actually came and talked, expressing enthusiasm for the new school, which infused us with the energy to keep going. It looked like the school would actually open.

> Still sits the schoolhouse by the road,
> A ragged beggar sunning.
> While round it still the sumac grows,
> The blackberry vines are running.
> **John Greenleaf Whittier**

School did open that fall with sixteen students. There were seven Garlands. Five of them were Peter and Mary's children; two were ours, and though our son was not in school, he participated in everything up until his nap time. Because a third of the school called us Uncle Jay, Aunt Toni, Dad or Mom, we ended up being called Aunt Toni and Uncle Jay. Many years later, it became Jay or Toni. I always said it is not what you say but how you say it.

One family, the Steeles, had six children, two of whom attended The Well that first year. The mom, Alice, referred to each day as the "daily drama" as well one might, being a widow with six children. Alice was an incredible resource for teaching materials. She introduced us to Ramalda Spalding's *The Writing Road to Reading*, a phonics program that we used for thirty-five years. That wasn't our only approach to teaching reading, but Spalding's program certainly provided an excellent beginning for young readers, allowing them to read real books within a very short time. Two other families made up the initial core of the school, the Eldredges and the Bauhans.

All of these families gave us remarkable support and reassurance. R.M. Eldredge initiated the recorder program, finding rich and beautiful music for the children to play. The program continued under the direction of other dedicated parents when R.M. retired, and then, as life sometimes designs, recorder teaching came back full circle and today is under the direction of one of R.M.'s daughters who was a first year Well student. The warmth and gratitude Jay and I felt then and still feel today for these families cannot be overstated. By some miracle it was just the beginning of a whole parade of talented, dedicated families.

We divided the group of students in half, eight for Jay and eight for me. The school and our home were one and remained so for thirty-four years. Our dining-room, our kitchen, our living-room, etcetera were open to all on weekdays and for our family during the rest of the time.

School opened at 8:30 and classes started at 9:00 in those days. The opening time was changed in later years to accommodate families with two working parents, but in the '60s, most families at The Well had one provider and a stay-at-home mom.

With the dead elms crowding the house, there was no open area for the students to play in other than the dirt driveway, so recess-time was used to clear land. And clear we did. Jay bought Swiss saws, axes, and cross-cut saws for all of us, and everybody set to, felling the enormous dead elms that stood all around the house. There were two nearly overgrown fields, one to the south and another to the north of the house. Both were covered with large birches and bushy, white pines. At recess, we could hear the kids singing and chanting, saws humming, and Jo or Mars yelling "Timber!" Down would come an elm, crashing to the ground. Kids scattered in all directions, then rushed back to "limb" and pile brush. No one was hurt. It was just more evidence of Superior protection at that time which I attributed to great luck. I did begin to suspect that we had landed on holy ground. Later on in life, I realized that there is no dumb luck and that all ground is hallowed.

I was also to learn that Spirit was involved in everyday activities, not just major decisions. But in those early Well years, many good things were attributed to fantastic flukes of fortune. The fact we cleared land for years with no major catastrophes had to be living proof.

When kids weren't sawing and chopping down trees at recess, they were building. Everyone wanted animals, so a shelter had to be constructed. Jay had gotten a load of rough cut lumber to be used not only for the animal shelter, but also for tree houses. Now, I am not talking about your ordinary tree house. These houses were way up in the air. It was a long climb up to them by the board ladders that were nailed into the trunks. The kids, boys and girls alike, hauled the boards up by pulley and built multilevel constructions. Some had porches; all had windows and doors. At the end of the school day, parents were led around by their proud children to view the latest drawing, plan, or project. The enthusiasm of the parents and the excitement of the children was phenomenal. Energy begot energy; enthusiasm begot enthusiasm.

Our first poetry recital and baking contest were held during the fall of the first school year. They generated a great deal of excitement. The fathers were willing to forgo work to attend. We all hated to miss a good dessert in those days, especially if it were concocted by a student. I had eight students, including a child of my own, to prepare for poetry recital. Students delivered their poems, standing in front of the fireplace in the living room. With each delivery, my heart thumped wildly. The pits of my arms were a puddle. Inwardly, I said and felt every word of all the poems. Of course, each child knew every other child's piece as well as they knew their own, a bonus I hadn't factored into the experience.

Little lamb, who made thee?
Dost thou know who made thee?
William Blake

When our child, Kambrah, recited William Blake's, "The Lamb," my heart pounded. I wept, choked back tears, and tried to act as if it were old hat. I tried to control my bursting pride, and of course, I couldn't. None of the parents could. The whole program was a hit. From then on, poetry recitals were scheduled three or four times a year for the next thirty-four years. To this day, at the first poetry recital of each year, one can see and feel new parents experiencing awe, pride, and nervousness as their children publicly recite their poem for the first time. The breadth and depth of the poems that the kids, their parents, and teachers chose over the years was impressive. The commanding stature and relaxed poise the children developed by reciting poems at The Well was apparent each time a child acted in a play, participated in a debate, or played in a music program. Jay and I loved poetry. How lucky to have a wealth of it recited regularly; it enhanced every year.

That first fall in 1967 was a busy one and stands out most vividly. Fridays, the students often spent the night. We burned brush, slept outdoors by the fires, sang, and watched the stars. Loving the heavens, Jay encouraged the kids who wanted to learn about the constellations or to just witness the beauty of the night to spend the night.

Often on Saturday, we trouped off to Boston, to the Science Museum in the morning and the Children's Theater in the afternoon. We piled into our light green microbus with seats replaced with hay bales to make space to accommodate more passengers. We seemed to sing everywhere we went—work songs, madrigals, folk songs, and the endless verses of "Oh, they built the Ship Titanic." (I revisited the "Titanic" song last year and was horrified at the brutality of the verses and the gusto with which we had sung about lives being lost and a ship sinking.) We definitely looked like hayseeds as we piled out at the Boston Garden. Well, actually, we were hayseeds. One thing I did notice, however, was that our children were among the most considerate and best behaved wherever we went. Their ages ranged from five to twelve. The older boys often had the younger ones in tow, crossing streets, standing in line, or looking at exhibits. Keven could be seen with Danny on his shoulders, going from one place to the next.

At the Science Museum, we would all agree to meet at the main desk at say, 11:30 A.M. At 11:30, all the students would be there. By 11:45 we would have to page Jay: "Would the director of The Well

I do not love him because he is good, but because he is my little child.
Rabindranath Tagore

Oh let's go up the hill and scare ourselves, As reckless as the best of them tonight By setting fire to all the brush we piled With pitchy hands to wait for rain or snow.
Robert Frost

Talk of mysteries! Think of our life in nature—daily to be shown matter, to come in contact with it—rock, trees, wind on our cheeks! The solid earth! The actual world! The common sense! Contact! Contact! Who are we? Where are we?
Henry David Thoreau

please come to the main desk. His school is waiting." Each time this happened, and it did happen more than once, you can imagine how delighted the kids were to catch Jay.

Come forth into the light of things;
Let nature be your teacher.
William Wordsworth

So many things from that first year became traditions, such as the love of and the importance of art and nature. Patsy Wilkens, a wonderful English woman, came to The Well with her three children, two of them school-age. She taught an unbeatable combination of nature and art class. She had a fondness for and a vast knowledge of bees which she imparted to the children through art , observation, (Jay set up a window hive), and study. The children crafted their favorite tree trunk—maple, oak, or pine—out of cardboard and papier-mâché. Inside, they constructed hives, complete with drones, workers, a queen, honey, and royal jelly. All eight grades worked on these hives. The information was contagious and spread among all the students.

Danny, a little first-grader, already had a working knowledge of bugs, one of his favorite items to collect. The respect that Danny gained from some of the older students because of his interest and knowledge about insects was marvelous to witness. Patsy became known as "The Bee Lady," and because of her classes, we always looked forward to Tuesdays and Thursdays.

When I think of that sunny corner classroom that housed those eight children and me, I know that I was totally privileged. My class consisted of my daughter Kambrah; three of her cousins Sarah, Tasha and Daniel; Danny and his brother, Matt; Ra, Bonnie, and another Sarah. Watching our five-year-old learn and play with her classmates in our own home were things that held tremendous value for me. I think that the incredible respect that I feel for my daughter Kambrah was established that year.

All through her earlier childhood, we knew that she was incredibly bright; she talked (she spoke Eskimo and English), she walked, she sang on key, and she memorized poems and books, earlier than most. Plus, she was exceptionally beautiful. All these gifts were hers, and then for me to discover that similar gifts existed in all the other children, as well, was an incredible realization. Each and every one of those children was outstandingly gifted. Yet each, too, was an average human being. Our daughter graciously let me see that and included these people in her heart, as well as generously allowing room for them in my heart. Her enthusiasm for school, friends, and community allowed me the freedom to have the same enthusiasm. In many ways, she was the spirit of The Well for me. It was she who led us to the realization that all children have incredible gifts—gifts that just need to be nurtured.

In the late fall of 1967, we did finish the animal shelter, complete with horrendous cases of poison ivy contracted by Jay and Matt, my little third-grader. They had been pulling out poison ivy roots from the foundation wall of an old barn cellar that was to be used as a side of the new animal shelter. It turned out to be very bad news. After a heinous bout with the rash that swelled faces beyond recognition, the shelter was completed.

Next we shopped for animals. We saw a pony and a donkey advertised in the *Weekly Market Bulletin*, a weekly farm news sheet. A farm in the nearby town of Rindge was selling the animals very reasonably. They had to be reasonable as we had no, I mean no, extra capital. Maybe they were even free, I can't remember. In any case, a few kids stayed after school to go with us to shop for animals and bring them home if they suited us. Again, we took out the middle seats in the Volkswagon bus and rattled over to the farm in Rindge. Now remember, both Jay and I grew up in a suburb of New York, so we had very little experience with animals other than dogs. My only background with large animals had been as a child, riding at a stable or visiting a farm in Michigan. No real knowledge in other words. None.

When we arrived at the farm, the round, jolly farmer brought out a donkey, Jenny, and a pretty little brown, black, and white pony, Kasha. It was immediate love at first sight on the part of everyone for the beasts, especially Packy, a fifth grader in Jay's class, who was smitten with the pony. The next problem was to get both animals in the bus. The farmer said, "I find that animals think with their stomachs," and he produced a coffee can full of grain. Yup. Into the bus they bounced. Next, all of us were holding halters and lead lines, crunched in the front and back seats.

That very premise Jay noted—"They think with their stomachs"—formulated the basis for "lunch tickets" later that fall. Jay would put five problems or so on the board for students to solve just before lunch, say go, and whenever they were done, that was their ticket to lunch. The speed, energy, and accuracy under those conditions was generally record-breaking.

With the animals in the bus, off we drove, feeling very successful. That feeling of success was short-lived. Within a mile of the farm, we ran out of gas. We were at the top of a long hill, and we could see a gas station, nestled at the bottom. Jay put the bus in neutral, and slowly we began to coast, the kids all chanting, "I think I can. I think I can." Slowly, we let out our breath. As the bus picked up speed, cheers picked up in volume. Neatly, we eased into the station, all of us smiling and high-fiving, certain that we had powered the vehicle to the pumps. We did get home safely, although it was clearly one more example of hovering angels. Those animals rode quietly the whole way, swaying gently with each curve, while Packy and Aaron passed handfuls of grain to them throughout the trip. We turned the animals out into their new home pasture, never realizing until much later how lucky it was that they hadn't kicked the doors out of the bus or anything else that might have been in the way. Definitely hovering angels. (Oblivion on our part.)

Our first summer at The Well, we acquired a calico Manx kitten, Bobtail, for Kambrah and a St. Bernard puppy, called Camel, for Ak. The kitten moved in easily, but Jay and I had more disagreements over the rearing of that dog than we ever had over any of the children. Camel grew to be a huge, long-haired, hundred-and-some-odd-pound mass with foot-long drools that flipped onto walls, furniture, and me whenever he shook his head, which was regularly. He was constantly fighting bouts with ear mites which made him shake his head violently. The dog quickly accepted our family as his, and he adopted all the first-year students at school, too.

Although the drools were sloppy and irritating, a more severe problem developed with Camel. He was not welcoming to anybody who was not included in his family.

The fall of the following year, we found ourselves lunging for him on a regular basis so that he would not intimidate the new arrivals by throwing his large mass at them while barking and generally being a nuisance. To some, he represented a source of great fear, peculiar for a school dedicated to love. His extended family was devoted to him. We tried endless ploys to get him over his distinct favoritism. I can still see Jay's tall, slim figure, bent over and disguised in odd clothes. I watched as Jay—a pot on his head, beating another pot with a wooden spoon—came around the corner of the house. He was hoping to have Camel charge at him so he could reprimand the dog on the spot and teach him that it was not good manners to mistreat strangers. This ruse never had a chance. I'm sure my mirth didn't help, because the dog knew instantly it was Jay and ran to him, tail wagging, drool drooling, and teeth bared in an enormous grin. We took the beast to dog-training school. No luck. It became clear that the dog had to go when he incarcerated our neighbor in his own house for a full day. That was the "straw" that broke the "Camel's" back. He had to leave. I was never so miserable in my whole life; we all were. There seemed to be a hole in the fabric of our family. And then, after a while, I felt incredible relief and freedom from the stress of an unreliable pet. The strain had been immeasurable.

We did learn a great deal from that experience. Looking back, I was surprised and ashamed at my smugness and the feeling of pride I felt at being part of the inner circle of that dog. I was later to witness that same combination of desperation and smugness in parents who had raised children whom only a mother could love.

It is not our preferences that cause problems, but our attachment to them.

Jack Kornfield

The metaphor of Camel became a useful reference for me. With a biting dog, you know with whom the dog is close. You! With an unruly or pouting child, one that only-a-mother-can-love and can comfort, the mother determines who may be close to her child—only herself. Unconsciously twisted, she creates and maintains the absolute dependence of her child. Only she may offer comfort. Only she may make demands. Only she can provide the right food. Only she has the recipe for sleep or can provide the right bed.

Of course, this is a natural and important job for the parents of babies, but if a mother does not allow other people to help care for and nurture the child, she causes the child to remain dependent upon her. She eventually has no authority and she loses control, leaving the child feeling destitute and isolated. I could see why one might raise such a child. We had raised just such a dog. We allowed Camel to undermine our own commitment of inclusion. We experienced the same blindness with a few students who charmed us at the same time they intimidated others. It is all such a delicate balance when working with a difficult individual. Excusing inappropriate behavior out of care and love, simply because the student is making progress, or seems to have a connection with a particular faculty member, undermines the integrity of the group, if there isn't some benefit to the group as well.

We were to find that theme often played out throughout the next thirty-four years and strangely, each time it seemed like it was new territory. Try as we would to establish protocol when dealing with difficult children, the guidelines seldom seemed adequate or fit the situation. Common sense tells you that inclusion and acceptance are basic ingredients for both a school's social development and a child's sense of comfort. Sometimes inclusion is not so easily achieved, and sometimes you don't even realize it is missing.

We have had students at The Well who seemed to love the school, and yet they did everything they could to be excluded. Some would break up games at recess, cry if they didn't get their way, hit, kick, get sent home, lose tempers, hog the swings or be a "dog in the manger," running and getting a swing so no one else could use it. Some made outrageous sounds in class. Some name called or teased people, subtly trying

The only real thing about affliction is the affliction itself- the cause of it is not a thing to be considered; the loss of a king's crown and a young girl's trinket weigh just the same in the scales of the Angel of Calamity.
Mark Twain

to hurt or sometimes overtly trying to hurt. Others loved to tell on people, just to get them in trouble. Some wouldn't do their homework or their class work. Some were disruptive in class. All of this was meaty material for class meetings and parent conferences.

The conferences were frequently as hard as some of the class meetings. Usually, students saw that they were interfering with harmonious work and play, and the group problem-solving strategy strengthened the school. There were students who took a long time to contribute positively, but who eventually made outstanding contributions to the community. There were other students who showed improvement, but their progress was too slow to warrant the price paid by the group.

Sheila was a youngster who entered The Well during her fifth-grade year. Her reputation had preceded her because she had known some of the Well students before she enrolled. She had a particular knack for stirring the pot and creating social havoc by being cliquish and generating feelings of exclusion among classmates. Sheila couldn't get her homework in on time, and she found it difficult to concentrate in class during the day. The "social" pre-empted every activity in which she partook. Her concern about with whom she sat or who was her friend-of-the-day colored the day for everyone. On a field trip, the car ride with friends was the highlight, not the museum, the play, or the planetarium. She could be found making social arrangements on the phone during job-time which negated any obligation to clean and broke the phone-use rule at the same time.

And yet, when she joined the drama group, she became alive and focused; she became a spectacular actress. Her ability to focus in the theater arts spread to art classes, where she became quiet, attentive, and able to surrender to the skills that the art teacher, Kate, offered. However, her general attitude in the rest of the academics remained

Good humored patience is necessary with mischievous children and your own mind.
Jack Kornfield

indifferent at best. Class meetings continued to center around this child. Relationships with students often remained difficult. She was a continual fly in the social ointment. It became clear that the give and take was way out of balance. So, at the end of the year, she was not asked to return to The Well. It was heartbreaking for us all. We had been sure that we could make this work. This child had potential and charisma. We wanted it to work. She possessed life, vitality, wit, and beauty, but the deceit and the chaos that accompanied those attributes eventually out-weighed the positive. It was time that the general good took precedence over the good of the individual.

On the other hand, there were students who, for a while, took up more than their fair share of time and energy, but by the time they graduated, they had given back to The Well community as much as, or more than, they had received. We had a little boy who attended The Well in kindergarten. He was a quiet, shy, slim child who loved to watch what was going on. He was well-liked by his classmates, which surprised me as he seemed to have the perfect personality for being teased.

Luke's family moved away at the end of his kindergarten year and then returned when he was in fourth grade. He was bullied once that year by a physically impaired third-grader, but I think that was the extent of the harassment he received. At that time, I wanted Luke to stand up for himself. It seemed odd to me that he would let a younger child take advantage of him. He wouldn't protect himself. He was simply a gentle child. That was before I understood that the best defense was to be undefended, something that Luke knew innately.

As a fourth-grader, he still was slim, quiet, and soft spoken. He was still an observer, but added to this were distinct facial tics, a slight stutter, and a spaciness that could be very distracting. He was subsequently diagnosed with Tourette's Syndrome. In class meeting, we talked about Luke's diagnosis and what we as a group could do to help. It is always such a delicate balance between helping someone or making someone more special. Pity cripples and undermines strength;

Nothing is so strong as gentelness, nothing so gentle as real strength.
St. Francis de Sales

Good weapons are instruments of fear.
Lao-Tse

compassion, much needed in everyone's life, let's one know we are here to help each other move forward.

"Special" falls into the pitying category, rendering the person helpless unless all the required conditions are met, generally an impossibility. We agreed, as a class, that we could do nothing for the tics other than ignore them, but we could help Luke focus; everybody could be useful. This group of children was remarkable. Mark, an excellent student and marvelous athlete, often sat next to Luke. Whenever Luke would drift off, Mark would gently pat his arm and remind him to come back. Sarah made sure he had his pencil, and Amara would get him on the right page. All this was done so subtly, it was hard to notice how skillfully these children were operating.

Luke's mom and I, hoping to glean some insight into the problem, attended a conference about Tourette's Syndrome. Many people who had Tourettes attended the conference and most were older than Luke. They blatantly exhibited some of the symptoms related to Tourette's. We were glad that Luke hadn't come with us. His expression of the syndrome was devoid of the strange sounds and foul language that was unwittingly uttered by the people at the conference.

Helen and I went home with real gratitude that Luke's case seemed so much more workable than many we had witnessed that day. More often than not, we are anxious and protective of our sons even when all seems to be well, but when something is seemingly amiss, the overprotection increases geometrically. Helen, Luke's mother, was no exception.

Of course she wanted the best for her boy, but trusting her child to the care of others, did not come naturally to her. Luke's obvious affliction expressed itself through tics and sporadic lack of focus (every one has some affliction, though it may not be as overt). His lack of focus made it difficult to determine when the affliction was the actual cause of incomplete work or when it was being used by him as an excuse for not completing required work. Any teacher who had ever worked with Luke knew he was a very capable student. We knew he could do the

In the middle of difficulty lies opportunity.
Albert Einstein

work. His parents, however, weren't as sure. At times, this made it difficult to agree on a plan for Luke.

Arrangements were made for Luke to have an after-school tutor so that he could get his homework done. This is frequently a good arrangement for a parent who has mistakenly taken on the child's homework and has inappropriately assumed the responsibility which belongs to the child. The parent-child relationship can relax in this area when the responsibility is clearly defined. We always encouraged parents to help their children, providing the experience was fruitful and pleasant for both parties. Parents can be a child's nearest and most interested natural resource. We encouraged these kinds of work-sessions. Yet even with a tutor, Luke still did not do his homework.

At the end of the summer, before going into the seventh grade, Luke decided not to return to The Well that fall. He hadn't done much, if anything, on his summer project. That probably weighted his decision about not returning. Procrastination was making decisions for him. Jay and I were very sorry; we'd miss his music, his interest in theater, but most of all, we would really miss him.

His mother went back to college that year to become acquainted with the latest ideas in educating special needs children. She relaxed when she found out that the expectations The Well had for Luke weren't excessive. Rather, the high expectations of The Well were in keeping with his abilities. He was a bright boy. Common sense.

Luke asked if he could return to The Well for his eighth-grade year. "Will you do the work?" Jay asked. He would. We were delighted to have Luke rejoin his class.

Occasionally, Luke still did not complete his work. In class meeting, Jay asked, "Are you willing to take responsibility for finishing all your work?" He nodded yes. Kate asked, "Do you want to be known as the boy with Tourette's or as Luke?"

"Luke," he replied with a smile, and Luke was how he was known. He made sure of it.

Not only did he stay for the next two years, completing eighth and ninth grades, but he excelled academically. He became an expert in the areas of Shakespeare and the Beatles. He gave four amazing performances as Prospero in a full-length production of *The Tempest*. He delivered his six hundred lines with perfect timing, in character. His hugs and gratitude at the end of each rehearsal, I am sure, still resonate within the theater walls as they do in my heart.

Today, he is finishing up his college degree, fluent in three languages, currently mastering a fourth. But more than that, he is one of the finest human beings I have known, still gentle, soft spoken, and retiring, except when he is on stage, of course. And guess what? No tics to speak of, or if they are there, no one notices. There is so much more to see.

The Well held more surprises for us. We initially thought that if we had a few boarding students, it would give us some extra income to defray some of the school costs and, at the same time, enhance the student body. Jay and I had taught at a boarding school for two years and had some ideas for improving the system that we had experienced. We thought that to have a large, family-type setting would be wonderful, an extended family for our own children and a healthy place for the boarding students.

We did have two boarding students that year. The first child to arrive, after school had started, was a little second-grader. Her mother settled her in, said a warm good-bye, and never returned. It took us two months to realize what had happened, and two more months to find the child's mother who was living quietly in South Boston. Though ordered by the court to come and get her child, the mom never appeared. Eventually the youngster became a ward of the town, and the town found a home for her. The family that she lived with wanted to adopt her but was thwarted by the mom, who after a few years reclaimed her daughter. I think it is just another day in the life of social services, but for us it seemed impossible that this could happen.

Our second boarder didn't last that long. He had nightly screaming fits, and his shrieks echoed throughout the house. After a week, we realized that our own kids were getting short shrift. The family setting that we had thought to offer was being eclipsed by these youngsters who were, in one case, abandoned and in the other so miserable that frequent tantrums were his regular outlet. So much for improving the system. We certainly were living, but were we learning? We decided that if we were to ever have people stay with us again, it would have to be the child's choice to attend, as well as the parents'.

The first year of The Well taught us so much and as busy as it was, it filled us up. The love and closeness we felt for those students was boundless and set a lovely precedent for the years to come. When I look back on it, I see huge snowdrifts (we had to get pay-loaders to get through the driveway that snowy winter). I can still picture the children, rosy-cheeked and exhausted, cuddled before the living-room fireplace, after skiing all afternoon at Whit's Ski Tow, a ski area just down the road from us. The sight of Ak, at three, flying down the hill on the front of Packy's skis, his red wool elf-hat sailing in the wind, took my breath away as a result of both joy and concern. We made bread for birthday cakes, we sang, we worked; there seemed to be children everywhere. The students' parents and grandparents supported our family and constantly encouraged us. Our own children's grandmother, Ursula, provided the Sunday respite—huge roast beef dinners. After dinner, we usually sat around the stone fireplace in her New Ipswich home, knitting, sewing, talking, and smoking. In those days we all were smoking, except Oma. Sometimes friends joined the Sunday meals, but mostly it was aunts and uncles and cousins. Often, children fell asleep in front of the fire, only to be wrapped in Oma's cozy down comforter or wool blankets and carried later to frosty cars. I knew then as I know now that we were totally blessed, strengthened, and nourished, wrapped in a wonderful life.

Do what you love.
Ursula Garland

That spring, Jay and I asked each other the question we were to ask each spring for the next thirty-four years, "Do we want to do this another year?"

"Yes, let's run the school for another year. It seems like a wonderful thing to do." And then we would send out requests for deposits. "No deposit, no return."

The summer of 1968, Jay found a shed for sale for fifty dollars. "What a deal," he assured me. "Since we know nothing of building, this can be our onsite workshop. We can take it down carefully; then it will be easy to re-assemble." I had my doubts and somewhere in the back of my mind, I wondered if I wanted to learn something of building, but take it down we did, and then we trailered it piece by piece back to The Well. We pulled every nail and replaced it with a new one later, on the new location. It wasn't rebuilt completely until the middle of the fall. By then everybody had worked on it. Katy, our kindergarten teacher, and I could be found after school cutting boards for the siding. Moms stopped to help. The kids nailed tarpaper onto the roof. This was our second animal shelter, and it served pretty well until, years later, a line wind ruined it by felling huge white pines, crushing the roof and uprooting the ground all around.

That shed housed ponies, chickens, goats, and sheep. There was a bunny, too, but not for long, because someone left the door open. It escaped from the shed but continued to live under it. The bunny and the donkey became great friends. In the early morning, you could see them rubbing noses, or sometimes when Jenny, the donkey, was lying down, the bunny would sit right on his back, cozy as could be.

Summers—full of land-clearing, building, painting, writing course study, swimming, and haying—presented a nice change of pace from the school year. Tons of roast beef and piles of strawberry shortcake, provided by Oma during the two weeks or so of haying, set a lovely tone for the summer. Adults and children worked, laughed and ate together, finally falling into exhausted heaps on the grass at the end of the day. It was then that we examined the prickle marks the hay bales had made all over our arms and legs. Only the children had enough energy to play croquet before the light gave way to the dark and the fireflies were the only source of light left. Cousins' and friends'

You-all means a race or section
Family, party, tribe, or clan;
You-all means the whole connection
Of the individual man.
Anonymous

overnights, either at our house or at theirs, danced their merry way throughout the vacation.

One summer, Jay put up a huge army-green canvas tent, the kind that has its own distinct musty aroma. He set it up on the little field at the side of the house, far enough for adventure, and close enough for comfort. Our kids, Kambrah and Ak, slept in it regularly, slowly emptying their bedrooms of essential articles and meticulously housing them in the tent. Often their cousins, Sarah and Tash, joined them. *Stalking the Wild Asparagus* in hand, they looked for wild edible food and cooked it over their little hibachi. They ate a lot of fried lambs quarter and garden peas that summer. Fortunately, the garden had plenty of early peas and snow peas. That old musty tent, housing our two children and their cousins, was kept far neater than any of their bedrooms ever were. Things were hung up and organized. A child could even be seen giving regular sweepings to the tent floor. We noted that ownership promoted care, responsibility, beauty, and pride.

I wonder now if children can do those things any more. Summers for children have become so much more structured, and safety is such a high priority. Anything that appears to be a risk, won't be covered by insurance. Today, companies dictate what you can and cannot do—have animals or build swings, jungle gyms, and tree houses.

When I was a young woman, a man came to the door selling life insurance. That, in itself, amused me, as I was young, and the notion made more sense to me that an older life was more in need of insurance than a young one. I said, "No thank you," to the insurance agent. He saw our two young children playing inside and whispered, "Well, I'd better not tell you, then, what every young widow knows," and he nodded grimly. I thought he was playing dirty-fear-pool. I smiled. "Do I get the insurance if I bump off my husband?" I inquired. Shaking his head, he left disgruntled. No sense of humor, I thought.

Something else that factors into present day fear is the concept of safety first. I ask you, with safety first, what can follow? What, but

Most of the luxuries, and many of the so-called comforts of life are not only not indispensable, but positive hindrances to the elevation of mankind.
Henry David Thoreau

pablum, can follow?(!) Modern generations have been watched and monitored from birth to the present moment. They can't get hurt. It's not in the job description. Because of the two-working-parent households, babysitters and daycare providers are a large part of childhood. The job of caregivers is to watch and keep safe and entertain. This is a very different atmosphere from one where a parent has a project that a child does along with him, or the child plays beside the adult activity, checking in from time to time. Today, as children get older, they spend their time in school, camp, or organized activities, where they are helmeted, seat belted (except on school buses), and lined up.

For me, the interesting question is do we know what makes a person feel safe? I don't think taking precautions removes all the risks. To me, it's the connection with the Spirit, the sense that there is a higher part in myself to rely on that eases anxiety. When I am not in touch with that, anxiety and fear have a chance to gain power, and when anxiety and fear enter, decisions are poor. Hence, we feel the need to buy more insurance, but are we any safer?

The Well provided that challenge for me regularly. Where would I find security, inside of myself or outside of myself? Were we taking unnecessary chances? To see people as capable and empowered was a constant challenge, especially when that wasn't how they were seeing themselves. An often repeated dining room table discussion among faculty and parents centered on the interrelated issues of self-reliance and safety. I don't think one can help children unless one sees them as complete and whole human beings. Seeing them as anything less only confirms their own fears.

When the school doubled in size the second year, inclusion became a major issue. It is just common sense to include and value everybody in a community. It may seem like an oxymoron for a private school to promote the idea of inclusion since the tuition alone implies separation of those who can pay from those who can't. By arranging work exchanges with parents, however, it was our intention and practice to make it possible for any student to attend The Well. To include new

I will fear no evil, for thou art with me.
Psalm 23:4

students was key, but remember, even our dog wouldn't make room for some of them. Camel may have expressed, in his own way, the school's conflict over inclusion.

Inclusion is the act of honoring the divine in man's nature. To honor the divine allows us to experience the connectedness to each other and to feel the brotherhood of man. In yoga, when we bow and chorus the word "Namaste," we are recognizing and acknowledging the higher purpose in our fellow man and the higher purpose in ourselves that allows us to connect. Even if only for a few moments this higher energy is brought to consciousness, it reminds us that the possibility of being inclusive is ever present. In fact, it is in our best interest. Each time we remember to be in touch with this higher force in ourselves and in others, we return to the foundation for order. "The environment may change, but man's needs stay the same," states the *I Ching*. Inclusion is a vehicle for meeting these needs. In order to be truly inclusive, we must learn to honor the divine in ourselves first and then in others.

My first memorable experience of inclusion was as a child in church groups. We were all not only encouraged to pray for ourselves, others and the universe, but we were encouraged to work together as a unit, doing dishes, setting up and cleaning up for church functions, singing and studying together. I adopted that model for my life. My connectedness established a sense of safety and comfort that I looked for as an adult, a life that promoted inclusion.

Truth is within our selves...
There is an innermost center in us all,
Where truth abides in fulness; and to know
Rather consists in opening out a way
Whence the imprisoned splendor may escape
Than in effecting entry for a light supposed to be without.
Robert Browning

By not separating ourselves, we gain connectedness with the whole, even when opinions, styles, or thoughts, may differ. The underlying force of respect continues to keep us joined in a positive way. All of us have a driving force to have our needs met. The key is to realize that the most basic of those needs is to connect through the heart rather than to separate.

My next encounter with intentional but limited inclusion came in the latter part of college. Jay and I were married at an early age, nineteen, and we thought that it would save a great deal of money if we were to live with some other friends—a couple and their child, and a single man. They were college classmates of Jay's. That period was one of the most intense but most wonderful of times for me. We shared a house together and learned to live and let live (most of the time), while we found ways of working through our differences. Hot and heavy gripe sessions were called at a moment's notice to resolve pent up feelings and solve problems. They were probably a precursor to class meetings at The Well, and they helped to achieve harmony in our little community. More often than not, the situation didn't change much at all, but the perception of the situation did, relaxing the atmosphere and allowing us all to breathe more freely. Learning to confront conflicts before they snowballed was a life lesson in itself. The environment doesn't need to change, but the perception of the environment does in order to move forward. We always have a choice as to how we will look at circumstances.

After we graduated from college, Jay and I moved to Barrow, Alaska, to teach for the Bureau of Indian Affairs (BIA). This whole experience became a play in contradiction. Naturally, we thought that the Bureau's job was to be inclusive. We found it to be the opposite. We were to teach the Eskimos, but we were not to "mix" with them. That seemed like the dumbest notion we had ever encountered. The underlying idea was that native people, according to the BIA, would never be able to run their own schools, churches, or government, implying that they didn't have the god-given wherewithal to manage their lives.

We, of course, learned from the Eskimos far more than we ever taught them, but we did have to honor them and join with them to learn it. We found the students extremely bright and resourceful. We loved Barrow, but we had serious doubts about BIA motives and beliefs.

> If a teacher is not respected,
> And the student not cared for,
> Confusion will arise, however clever one is.
> This is the crux of the mystery.
>
> Lao-tse

When looking at something of wonder, a bug or a picture, we saw students lean into each other with guttural utterances, "Ahza!"

At other times, they would stay up all night to work on a school newspaper. Raw interest and enthusiasm electrified the group. Group connectedness, regular physical contact, and intimacy was a way of life for these children. Awareness of community needs played a strong part of everyday life. They helped older people "pack" or carry water, split wood and haul ice. Inclusion was what we were looking for in our own lives.

In Barrow, a village of about 1500 in 1960, we witnessed the love children had for each other and for their parents. They showed us how an entire community could be inclusive. It was easy for us to have this connection with the students; however, our contact with the adults in that village was very limited.

It was only when we moved to a smaller village on the Lower Yukon that we had a fuller picture of inclusion in terms of the whole community, adults as well as children. There we were privileged to know not only the students, but their parents and grandparents, as well. There we taught students who also loved to learn. They loved to be at school. Often it became a haven for them, a time and place free of drinking, fighting or shooting. The unique idea that children were welcome at any time in any home in the village to eat, spend the night, or just hang out, afforded a real sense of safety which was essential, especially since home was not always a safe environment. The people of Pilot Station loved babies. Anybody's child was welcomed, yours or theirs. Our children were welcomed all over the village. Kids watched out for kids. There existed a pride and discipline in children that I had rarely witnessed before.

All of the children had manners. It astounded me that the kids resisted grabbing for food when it was offered. Instead, they took moderate servings, no matter how hungry they were. If a little one were tempted to over-do in serving size, an older brother or sister was right there to set him or her straight.

There was a connectedness throughout the village that I had never experienced on such a large scale before. There were, of course, drawbacks to this closeness that became apparent the longer we stayed. A strong community can be confining if you have a desire to enlarge your personal community. That pressure from the community made it hard for those who wished to expand their horizons and leave. Fundamentally, love and care permeated the village, despite the fact that this was a tough village with a high degree of alcoholism. Even so, the power of inclusion and community was strong. It made an enormous impression on me, and I knew it was something that I wanted in my personal and my teaching life.

At The Well, we continually tried to encourage students to be inclusive. We realized that this was more likely to occur when the children were most comfortable with each other. Often, in the fall, the Upper School, grades five through eight, and faculty and chaperones would go to a camp for a week. The camp was owned and run by a Well family, and they let us use the facilities. Susan, the mom, headed up the kitchen, creating inspirational meals from the ingredients that our students brought. Each cabin constellation comprised a teacher, two fifth-graders, two sixth-graders, two seventh- and two eighth-graders. Of course we did this to mix up any existing cliques. The melding of grades allowed them to get to know each other better.

One year, Jay decided to give everybody a new name for the week. He thought that this exercise would give us a chance to look at each other a little differently, if only for a while. It was with glee and hilarity that we accepted our new appellations. Trying to remember new names of old friends did slow us down a little. The rule: no one could answer unless you used their new name. It was a wonderful way to start off a week, all of us working hard to memorize the thirty-five or so names, making acquaintances with old friends in a new way.

One of the mom-chaperones was not in favor of this at all and felt ridiculous with her assigned tag. It made it all the more comical to have an adult refuse to participate in the game. Naturally, the kids picked up on this immediately, and they enjoyed witnessing an adult having a mini-tantrum. Agreed, Clytemnestra is not a handle one

All things are connected...Whatever befalls the earth, befalls the children of the earth.

Chief Seattle

would readily pick for oneself; eventually she gave up her resistance and joined in. Actually, at dinner, she needed the butter passed and had no alternative but to use the new names. Another example of the motivational power of food.

The second year of The Well held other new experiences, including evening play readings with parents and students and contra dancing. Dudley Laufman came with his fiddle and accordion; Bob McQuillan played accordion, Kay Gilbert, the flute; and sometimes Newt Tolman joined in with another flute. The dances were held at the Eldredges' barn studio or in the Haddocks' living room at Brush Farm. Those evenings seemed to be an animated Currier and Ives picture. As they stepped carefully up the snowy paths towards the house—no one shoveled in those days—the women and girls bustled along in their long skirts and snow boots. The boys hopped from one drift to the next. R.M. or Libby, depending upon which home we were dancing in, greeted us at the door and the fiddle music filled the winter air. It set a lovely stage.

Choosing partners could also lead to uncomfortable feelings, so everyone had to have a new partner for each dance. These attempts to mix didn't totally ease the dilemma of the wallflower, but everybody did dance, which was a beginning.

Katy Barnes was a strong force in supporting our ideal of inclusion. Katy started a kindergarten class at The Well in which our son, Akhil, was a student. He joyfully built a birch bark tipi, birch bark bowls, and birch bark spoons. Ak was so motivated that he provided our whole family with birch bark tableware. Eating cereal in the morning took some extra time, given the bowls were tippy and the spoons sometimes leaked. It hadn't been easy finding a lot of straight twigs, so the spoon handles bent in directions that made it difficult to predict just where the bowl of the spoon would settle. We all were part of the project.

Katy moved to the first grade the following year as did Ak. I heard Ak and Kambrah talking in their bunk beds the night before Ak's first day in first grade. Kambrah reassured him for quite some time, telling him all would be well and the new class wouldn't be much of a change from the year before. He would get to spend the full day in school and he would learn to read. Akhil had been everybody's darling in the whole school for two years and had been included in every activity. He was carried up mountains on Daniel's shoulders, pushed on the swings, and placed as a passenger on the front of Aaron's or Packy's skis. I guess we had overdone the idea of his being a "big boy" and going into first grade, because, there he was, having been read to and safely tucked into his bed, telling his sister he was really "wow-wied" about 'fust' grade. (For his first seven years Ak spoke like John Kennedy. He was missing many of his Rs.) It was surprising to me to realize the anxiety he had. Even though Katy had been his kindergarten teacher, one he knew and loved, even though his new class was in the same room as the year before, and even though his classroom was in our house, he was nervous about life in first grade.

The next morning he wouldn't wear his new school clothes. He said he wanted to save them until he "liked" school again. That, incidentally, was the following day. Ak let me have a wonderful window into an anxious place for a child that I would never have considered. Our children did that for us regularly. Clearly, the first day of school is a big event for each child, but I had never realized just how big. What to an observer seems old and familiar, may not seem old and familiar to some one else, because it has taken on a new meaning.

Katy had an excellent sense of children's literature and had the little first-graders reading "real" books in no time.

Katy stayed at The Well, teaching and enhancing a wonderful first and second grade program. She provided The Well with her two children, and she provided us with a wonderful friend and colleague for the next seventeen years.

Because our school was so small, we needed all of the students to participate in everything: soccer, plays, dancing, and singing. And this need was answered by the idea of inclusion. Katy jumped right in and

The man who does not read good books has no advantage over the man who can't read.
Mark Twain

became involved with everything, as did her children. Jay, Katy, and I would wolf down our lunches to get out and have lunchtime soccer and Eskimo baseball games with the kids. We all skied, cleared land, fed animals, contra danced, and laughed a lot, really a lot, together. Faculty continued to participate in everything in the years to come.

The second year perpetuated the traditions that were established in the previous year. The first year of anything seems to establish traditions. "We always did it this way," the kids would tell us. I wondered how once or twice, could become a tradition, but it surely was in the kids' minds. For the new students, getting the hang of the traditions wasn't always easy.

Poetry recitals had become a fixed tradition, so as our first poetry recital came around in the fall of our second year, youngsters practiced their poems and inadvertently learned each other's. Ephraim, a new student in the third grade, approached his with a gusto only he could muster. He was a stocky boy with a head of curly hair and an aptitude for pure dedication and perseverance when something caught his imagination. The flip side of his perseverance was a stubbornness of equal intensity that he expressed by digging in his heals, snorting and pacing, and occasionally losing his temper when something did not tickle his imagination. His choice of poem, "Mommy Slept Late While Daddy Fixed Breakfast," by John Ciardi, clearly intrigued him. He learned it quickly and appreciated the humor in it every time he recited it. His infectious enjoyment spilled over into the class.

We were all thoroughly prepared with our poems when the recital day arrived. The living room was too small to accommodate all the students, parents, and friends the second year. The performance was held in Jay's classroom, the largest room in the house, and a low first-grade table became the stage. Word had spread that these programs were totally enjoyable and not to be missed. Thus, there were many adult friends in the audience. Each child hopped up on the table, one at a time, and recited his or her poem. Things went smoothly until it was Ephraim's turn. "Ephraim", I said. Silence and no movement. "Ephraim, it's your turn," I said. Still no movement. By now, the entire room was transfixed. The room seemed filled with an overwhelming silence. Not a muscle moved anywhere. You could feel the tension mounting. Unsure what to do, I decided to call the next person to relieve the tension. I feared if I did, though, we'd go through this again, or Ephraim would never say his poem in public, which would be a shame since he loved it so. "Ephraim," I said again. There was a snort from Ephraim's direction and a scuffle of feet. I looked to see if he were leaving the room. No, just changing position. I said his name again. More snorts, more scuffling of feet, the entire room was still frozen. Jay went over, picked up Ephraim and placed him on the table. Bright red in the face, curls damp with perspiration, breathing completely out of sync, Ephraim huffed out the title of his poem "Mommy...Slept...Late...While...Daddy...Fixed...Breakfast." A long pause ensued. There was more heavy breathing and a few snorts, but then the name of the poet followed. Ephraim heaved and sighed through the poem and paused to take some deep breaths. With every new verse, the audience, too, began to breathe. When the final line was said, the cheers and applause could be heard in town, I am sure. Ephraim leaped off the table, the victor. He knew he had conquered something beyond the recitation of a poem. At the next poetry recital, he recited "Paul Revere's Ride" with perfection and a gusto that only Ephraim was capable of mustering.

The Haddocks joined us that winter, in the middle of the school year, enrolling their son in the first grade. They were drawn to The Well because their little first-grader, Joey, was not learning to read. Actually, the publication of *Why Johnny Can't Read* had recently made people aware of a national reading problem. In many school systems, phonics had been deleted from the curriculum, and its absence was taking a toll. Fortunately for us, by using Alice Steele's Ramalda Spalding program, coupled with a Lippencott program (which we used less and less as time went on), all our children, including Joey, did learn to read.

The highest point a man can attain is not Knowledge, or Virtue, Goodness, or Victory, but something even greater, more heroic and more despairing: Sacred Awe!
Nikos Kazantzakis

And a little child shall lead them.
Bible, Isiah 11:6

Joey influenced me a great deal. He loved his life and continually showed it. The gratitude that he expressed for his existence was mind-blowing and it continued right through all of his years at The Well. He was a constant reminder to be grateful. He was an amazing artist, illustrating the things we read in school—the Greeks, the Bible, the Romans, fairy tales, and myths—with remarkable drawings. He loved his animals: horses, ponies, chickens, and goats. His style was slow and easy, mixed with helpfulness and mirth. Great combination! Our students taught us a great deal and often pointed a way when we couldn't see one clearly ourselves. All of the Haddock family brought tremendous energy, humor, and spiritual wealth to our school, but it was Joey who led the way. Children often do that for us, if we can only let it happen.

A core of committed parents and teachers developed during the second year. Families working together and playing together produced quality times and wonderful memories. The dining-room table became an after school gathering place for parents and faculty to visit with each other. Endless cups of tea and coffee were consumed, as we talked about children, husbands, relationships, and school. Everyone struggled with daily dramas, yet everyone laughed. Most felt relieved to discover that they weren't alone in seeking balance in love, in discipline, in work, and in play. The trick was always to see each other and our children as whole, complete, and capable. Sometimes that required a lot of work. There were some very heavy, and some very hilarious, conversations about the path to get there. Parents and faculty grew in understanding and learned from each other.

Yet, the children seemed to surpass us. They seemed to move with lightning speed as we slogged along, often caught up in unimportant details. I am not, however, in any way, belittling our great discoveries. It is the coffee times, the everyday moments between events, not the events themselves that often create the quality of life.

Widdie Iselin, a young woman from Nelson, New Hampshire, came to The Well early that first summer, looking for a job. She was of medium height, and a slender build but one that implied real muscle and strength. Her most impelling physical characteristic was a broad, impish smile with glistening white teeth. Widdie was to become an integral part of our early Well family and an important part of our immediate one. She hoped to teach French, but of course, we weren't in a financial position to pay ourselves, so certainly we could not hire anyone else. She continued to work at Monadnock Architects, a company created by Jay's brother, Peter, and Art Eldredge. We discovered Widdie to be full of life and daring, always ready to explore creative avenues. Widdie was adored by our two children. She rented "The Love Nest," a little log cabin across the road from The Well. It had no running water, but it did have a cold-water indoor pump. She showered at our house and often stayed for supper. In those days, people could live in the woods without amenities and borrow the ones they missed.

Widdie had moved next door at the right time for us; Jay and I were expecting our third child. As my pregnancy moved along during the summer of '69, I began to be concerned about the combination of teaching and motherhood. How would there be time for it all with a new baby coming?

"No problem," said Widdie. "I love babies. I'll quit my job and come help you out." She did love babies and was consumed with the idea of having her own. Repeatedly, I reminded her it would be better to have a husband first. I was never really sure that she believed me. Now I question the validity of that statement myself.

Unbelievable, I thought, with instant relief. Although she didn't quit her job until after Danda was born, she helped me all summer, stopping by after work. Jay's sister in California was moving, and he had gone out to help her. Widdie stayed with the children and me. Daily, I grew larger in girth. We gardened, made a tile-topped coffee table, swam, relaxed, and did summertime things with the kids.

Ursula, Jay's mother, was also very much on hand that summer. Actually, she was available every summer. That was a given. She was a great family field-tripper, ready at a moment's notice to pile kids in our little Volkswagon bug (or hers) and off we'd go. Often, the cousins would join us. There were no seat belts in those days, so the two smallest kids wedged themselves into the well, a space behind the backseat. The other three were in the backseat, and Ursula and I were in the front.

It could be the Sunapee Arts and Crafts Fair, the circus, or the beach, but whatever it was, she was up for it. Somehow she was always totally prepared with chewable vitamin C tablets, carrot sticks, cheese, and green grapes to ward off hunger pangs; blankets for the cool evenings; Kleenex and Band-Aids; and songs. A favorite song was "Hop hop hop, pferdchen laut gal of. Über stich, und uber steine, ...," a German children's song. If worse came to worse, there was a reserve of chocolate on board, somewhere. You never knew when you might be stuck in a snowbank and need sustenance. You never knew when all of the kids might fall asleep and you could slip a chunk in your mouth. Ursula was a master at that. Of course, she had to be with her incurable yen for the stuff. "It's good for me," she'd declare. This, coming from the mouth of the original whole-grain, natural foods promoter. I'd say nothing, but I had my reservations, because I knew it wasn't health food for me. (She died at ninety-five, still consuming thirteen huge Cadbury bars, each weighing a pound, every two weeks.) Many paths to good health!

The Monadnock Region was a rich setting for our school and family community. The Bolles had moved to Francestown and had two boys at The Well. Jim taught violin that second year along with solfeggio (a way of teaching music by assigning a name to each note, ie. do, re, mi). He and his wife, Jocelyn, had established Monadnock Music the year before. They developed a fabulous group of musicians who gave free concerts throughout the summer for area residents. Families were welcome, and since the town churches seated many, there usually was room for the children to stretch out and snooze halfway through the concert while the music continued.

Choose a job that you love and you will never have to work a day in your life.
Confucius

Let music loosen deafness to spirit. Play and let play.
Rumi

The summers were rich with wonderful things to do. The Monadnock Region embraced the arts and took second to none in natural beauty, prompting hikes on trails all around.

By the time school was about to start in the fall of our third year, I felt and looked like twins were in the offing. My stomach seemed to enter a room minutes before the rest of me. There was so much to be done daily; and somehow, all working together, we got it done. There were children and animals to be looked after, a garden to be tended, grass to be mowed, and wood to be cut.

When school began, homework started for us all, and we gathered around the dining-room table at night. Kambrah and Ak painted the cradle Jay had built for Ak when he was born, and they waited excitedly for the new babe to descend from the stars.

In late September, as my birthday approached, Jay, Kambrah, and Ak went shopping. Joyfully, they came home, all excited about their purchases but with nothing in hand. They made a lot of insider references to each other about their selection of a present for me. The day of my birthday arrived, along with two truckloads of trees and plants. Everybody was so delighted, pointing to where the fruit trees could go, and how, when the arborvitae grew, it would cover the boarded over windows on the north side of the house. I looked at all there was to plant, massaged the beach ball I had for a stomach, and barely fought back my tears. Seeing the joy in their faces, yet knowing the work it was going to involve getting these plants into the earth, I felt conflicted.

Today, those trees do touch the roofline of the

I attended The Well before I was old enough to go to kindergarten. I remember sitting under the table in Upper School French Class as my mother taught. I would listen to the fifth and sixth graders roughly recite from Jean de la Fontaine's Le Corbeau et Le Renard. (Even today I recall parts of the poem). It was during these early days that I first remember seeing Jay Garland. From the floor of my mother's classroom, through the hall into the next room, I could catch glimpses of Jay teaching the seventh and eighth graders. He seemed enormous. Furthermore, he taught with such enthusiasm and energy, that he would frequently shake, at which point he'd have to re-adjust his glasses on his nose. To a five-year-old, Jay was huge in height and in presence. In fact, I found him terrifying. Through the years this first impression would be transformed into a deep respect for a dignified, caring individual—he was more than a teacher, rather a mentor committed to sharing his spiritual strength and wisdom.

I would spend five years in the Lower School with Toni before I would find out what it was like to be in class with Jay. My memories from kindergarten through fourth grade are mostly filled from Toni's wonderful, infectious laugh. If something struck her as funny (which many things seemed to), the entire Lower School would know about it—if not from her laugh, from her familiar "Woo hoo!" Similarly, if a student misbehaved or didn't do their homework, Toni's reaction would have a lasting effect—first anger, then forgiveness. If I ever got in the latter situation, no matter how bad the moment felt, it always seemed to end with a hug. This reflected The Well School's home rule of discipline and love interwined.

Needless to say, Jay and Toni's Well School often strayed from the curricula and disciplinary action prescribed by many other schools. In fact many of the greater lessons taught and learned were outside of the classroom and even outside of a normal school day. My imagination, curiosity, and eagerness to learn were inspired by our participation in extraordinary extracurricular activities, and I don't just mean stacking wood!

186

We had access to everything to awaken our own passions in music, art, nature, or sports. I have fond memories of skating on the pond, planting bulbs around the school, bird watching, and beachcombing on Plum Island. I remember coffee houses, poetry recitals and countless plays and performances. In all the plays, whether on stage or behind stage, we were all encouraged to be anything and anyone–Rutledge, Prospero, Lucy, Huck and Jim, and even the "voice behind" Thomas Jefferson's wife! We learned about the community and then built our own "Peep town;" we cared for the animals (especially Gabriel) in the barn, and invented the costume closet. We even went West (west of Harrisville, that is). With every game, every song, every poem and every line, Jay and Toni were right there with us, either on the sidelines or in the front row, living the same experience with wild and supportive gestures or desperately trying to help if we couldn't remember our part. It's interesting that the teachers I once almost feared taught me to fear nothing, but to explore everything.

Larissa Khouw

house and they did indeed cover the closed-off windows. Each fall, for many, many years, we have enjoyed two kinds of delicious pears. The annuals did die, and the year that the peach tree began to bear, someone ran over it with a tractor. The cherry tree didn't make it either, as it was in the way of the waterline to the Upper Building. It didn't survive the transplant. There were a few casualties, but for the most part, growth and development reigned.

Even with all the help that we received from friends and family, we still had financial angst. There were still bills to be paid. Often I wondered just how we were going to do that, and then I would be reminded of Ursula's words: "Just do what you love and the rest will follow." Sometimes I wished it would follow a little more quickly.

I did believe her, though, and the rest did follow. For example, the first year, when we discovered we needed a new furnace, we worried about how to pay for it. Then a new student enrolled. Bingo, the bill was paid. It so often worked that way. I had to start reminding myself not to look at the new students as roofs or furnaces, windows or doors. I am continually grateful for the way things just work out. Worried? Give it to the Universe. The incredibly stupid thing is how many frenetic machinations I went through before I remembered: Ah, give it to the Universe!

We did have another student, Judy, live with us that year, but this time it was definitely her idea as well as her parents'. She was great and looked forward to the new babe with as much enthusiasm as our own kids. Judy hoped the delivery would be delayed to coincide with her birthday. Danda arrived right on time, October 16th, early Friday morning, not on Judy's birthday which was at the beginning of November. Thank heavens from my point of view.

Oma came over to run the household, while I was in the hospital.

Widdie had come at five o'clock to stay until Oma arrived, then she went to work. We called off school that day, and made it a holiday for all. The joy and ecstasy that Jay and I felt over the birth of a healthy little girl was overwhelming. The memory of lying there on that hospital stretcher, both of us laughing and weeping and hugging our newly arrived daughter is still very real today. We were filled with such gratitude for this new life. The kind of awe that a new child evokes is so inspirational that it raises the capacity for love beyond the imagination. You would think that we—all parents—would make a conscious effort to remember daily the feeling of this magnificence. Unfortunately the daily routine quickly eclipses the awe-inspiring and only allows time for brief glimpses of reflection into the miracle of life and what that holds. Each birth changes us all and offers the world so much.

Everybody appreciated the long weekend so much that it became the official Fall Break time for years to come. Jay had bought a case, yup, a case, of Stouffer's frozen macaroni to tide us over for the duration of my convalescence, a period of one and one-half days. His reputation of "by the case Garland" was just gelling. Even though he was never a Boy Scout, "It's good to be prepared", seemed to reverberate throughout every cell in his body. It makes you wonder, sometimes, how another person's mind works. Ursula came and helped for a week, making meals (not frozen macaroni) and generally keeping the home front going. She was wonderful. I remember plates piled high with juicy black, red, and green grapes. Sliced apples, always a healthy snack, or delicious drinks were magically placed within my easy reach. Ursula made certain my time could be devoted to holding and feeding our baby.

Walnut Acres, a natural foods mail order house, was high on our list for grocery shopping or ordering. Although foods from Walnut Acres were healthy, they weren't always tasty. A perfect example of that was Danny's Porridge, a whole-grain hot cereal that Ursula prepared each morning during her stay with us. Each child had a different description of its flavor: dog biscuits, ground horse feed, and so on.

Many recall, with mixed reviews, the natural peanut butter that hung or clung from the roof of your mouth long after the rest of the sandwich was digested.

In another natural foods household, Peter, Jay's brother, did eat a whole bowl of dry dog food and was going for seconds when Mary came into the dining room and made him aware of what he was eating. His comment was, "Actually, I thought it was a new and improved brand of whole-grain cereal." These whole grains were the fare in the '60s and the '70s, not that they aren't popular now, but the taste and presentation are far superior today.

Fruit leather—only available in Cambridge in the '60s—was usually apricot in flavor and was rolled out apricots. Mary, who spent a year in Turkey, informed us that it was "Probably flattened by dancing barefooted Turks." Today's fruit leather is primarily sugar and is sold in supermarkets nationwide. I would have to say it is candy although it is advertised as a "healthy" snack. The apricot fruit leather was the closest our kids ever got to candy.

Once a year, for about thirty years, we had "Health Week" at The Well. During these five days, only healthy foods could come to school. Soda, candy, and gum were always on the 'no' list, but in addition, no chemicals or refined sugar were permitted in the lunches, which pretty much outlawed all processed food. The students and teachers prepared healthy snacks for recess-break and talked about what made strong, healthy bodies. For some, their lunches remained much the same, but many students found it was difficult to figure out what to bring to school. Many yogurts, meats, and almost anything prepackaged couldn't be brought to school. There were groans throughout the Upper School, especially with the older children, as imagined sugar and chemical deprivation set in. Actually, it was only an eight-hour hiatus, since anything could be consumed before or after school. Every year, it was an eye-opener for the students and me, as we became aware of the additives that were in our everyday meals. Each year, there were more processed foods available. Of course, there is the idea that what comes out of your mouth is more important that what goes into it. But it is always important to be aware of both directions.

When we brought Danda home from the hospital two days later, we were greeted by a houseful of family, including our huge, drooling dog. Camel accepted Danda immediately and was very attentive to her. Now there is a mystery. He must have had a way of checking the DNA.

Danda went to school with me each day, except when she was sleeping. Her bedroom was just upstairs. The children carried her around, played with her, and changed her diapers. Some even wore extra sets of diaper pins attached to their shirts in case they were needed when changing the babe. We were always misplacing the pins. Cloth diapers soon took a back seat to the new paper inventions when we realized the advantages. Because we were such whole-grain, natural-fiber people in those days, it was embarrassing how quickly we caved in to the new disposable diapers. In those days, however, paper diapers, needed the same pins as the cloth; those handy closures that are available today were not on the market then.

Widdie left for the West later that fall after helping me with the new baby, and Libby Haddock came with her ten-month-old son, Raphy, to take care of Danda during crucial school hours. A favorite memory of mine was Raphy sitting on our old Farmall tractor, his pacifier clutched between his gums and hanging from the side of his mouth. He was grrring and whirring loudly, pretending to drive the dingy red vehicle all over The Well grounds. Our family, Well and personal, was expanding.

That winter, a group of interested parents and faculty met to discuss the possible creation of a high school. We needed new energy if we were to develop the next four grades. We invited discussion concerning the principles behind the high school. We wanted a large group of people to help formulate a mission statement. That sounds simple, and it probably could have been, but it wasn't. On Saturday nights, we would gather at someone's house, with a group of anywhere

Let us put our minds together and see what kind of world we can make for our children.

Sitting Bull

190

between fifteen and twenty people, and talk until the early morning. We identified what we had learned in high school that was valuable enough to pass on to the students of The Well High School. We were looking for truths, not just things that were true. And what were some of these truths?

All students have an abundant amount of creative genius.

The job of a teacher is to learn as well as teach.

Without care and love, criticism should not be delivered, because it is too hard to absorb.

Nothing is fair or everything is fair, however you want to accept it.

A classical curriculum that is heavily weighted in the arts provides a rich foundation for life.

Education should provide avenues for the genius in each child to be expressed through art, music, drama, math, and writing.

Those were some of the ideas we agreed upon. It took a lot of discussion and baring of the soul. These truths were similar to those we embraced for the elementary grades. From these long winter nights, and some spring ones too, came the decision to go ahead with a high school. We saw it as an extension of the existing school and hoped for enthusiastic involvement from the faculty, parents, and students. We wanted committed students who were willing to work hard and to put in the time to do well. We found a director for the high school, a friend who had taught with us when we worked at a small school in Deerfield, Massachusetts.

We needed a building for the high school. Roger and Barbara, Jay's brother and sister-in-law had moved to New Hampshire, and Roger was willing to be the general contractor. Barbara, Jay, and I were the crew. Bob, a student with incredible energy and good cheer, joined us early on. We were the slaves, and anyone who stopped by to check the progress became one too. No standing around.

In the summer of 1970, there were always people stopping by on their way from one commune to the next, looking for food and a place

One's mind once stretched, by a new idea never regains the original dimension.
Oliver Wendall Holmes

"Men work together," I told him from the heart, "Whether they work together, or apart."
Robert Frost

to sleep. (Remember, this was New Hampshire and it was just catching up to the '60s culture). In those days, there were communes all over the U.S. We encouraged people to help in exchange for a bed and breakfast, lunch or dinner. Those were the "beautiful people." They ate a lot and some sang; a few were actually helpful. Many just loved to sit and do nothing, a place that I am just getting to thirty-four years later. (It's a rather nice place.) Almost all of them were interesting to talk with, and most were enthusiastic about what we were doing but did virtually nothing to help out. They really had no concept of what to do. Practical knowledge had not been a priority with them.

We needed a new building that was inexpensive and could be built in sixty days, in time for school to open in the fall. We found a government design for a cabin with an ingenious heating system: Leave a small crack in the perimeter of the floor, blow the hot air under the floor and let it rise through the cracks between the floors and the walls. The plan called for a 24 x 12 foot single-story building; we modified the dimensions and came up with a building that was 24 x 96 feet. The shape resembled a railroad car. It must have been influenced by Jay's summer work on the California railroad when he was just out of high school or those New York City apartments that have all the rooms off one long hallway, except this had no room for a hall.

Keeping the construction low-cost was critical. So, for two precious weeks, Jay, Roger, Barbara, and I tried to hand dig holes for sonotubes. The cement-like hardpan finally wore out our hands and backs; we called in a backhoe. The foundation tubes were poured with cement. We erected the walls and placed the trusses we had ordered atop the 96 feet of the east-west walls. When the roof was completed, we put in insulation, ceilings, doors, and some windows, but fourteen sliding-glass doors down the south side of the building (we love light) had yet to arrive. We opened school on schedule without windows. Picnic tables served as classroom desks. This all sounds pretty step-by-step, one, two, three, but before we could even begin to build, we had to finish haying, so we didn't start building fulltime until after the 4th of July.

Our own children had needs, too. There were songs to be sung, bedtime stories to be told, and swimming holes to be investigated. There were often extra people for dinner. Huge pots of spaghetti or lasagna, large salads, endless pies and cookies, and heavy homemade bread, along with all the food from the garden, was the general fare—all served by candlelight. Candles made everything look and taste better, and for good reason, you couldn't see the food. Lunches were cottage cheese and strawberries (Oma and Grandad style), topped with sour cream, with any leftovers to fill in. To round out the meal, we had Walnut Acres peanut butter, bread, and honey, which stuck to our ribs. When I think of it now, I wonder how we moved after lunch. My brother once told me to cut the dining-room table in half if I ever decided to save money. Good reasoning, but it never happened.

Ak and Kambrah were building a fort in an old barn cellar next to the new high school building. They were using the leftover materials from the high school building for their construction. As each phase of the school was completed, they gathered materials to complete that stage on their house. When we put up the walls, they put up the walls on their place; when we roofed, they roofed. They had quite a fancy dwelling when it was completed.

Some of the drifters that came through were interesting. Word had gotten out so people continued to stop by our house the following winter as well. Some were just doing the commune circuit, going from place to place, staying for a while, then moving along. Most either walked or hitchhiked which was a very common mode of travel in those days. We all had "thumbed;" Jay and a friend had gone to California together "on their thumbs," the summer after they had graduated from high school. People traveling, coming through for a night or day, often had interesting tales to tell.

One person who visited and stayed with us had walked and hitched from Peru traveling from commune (or monastery) to commune. He was looking for "The Way" and was very wrapped up in G.I. Gurdieff and P.D. Ouspensky. I, being both a pragmatist and an opportunist,

Hitchhiking requires that you take what comes, that you learn to be sociable with all sorts of people, and that you be ready for detour and delay **Philip Simmons**

mentioned, "Our way is first we work, then we eat." He was happy to work and then moved along. I do wonder where all of those "beautiful people" who used us as a bed and breakfast are now.

Conval, a new, consolidated high school was opening up in our town that fall. Everything was state of the art. Everything was new with endless specialized classrooms and beautiful sports facilities. Don't you wonder why people would enroll in our high school with unfinished floors and gaping holes where windows ought to be? Yet, twenty students did enroll and paid tuition, as well.

It wasn't long before two of the new high school students were living with us. The commute from Keene was too long, and they wanted to participate in many of the after school activities. They would just get home and have to turn around and come back. Did we ever learn? Somehow, we always had people living with us. Someone suggested that boarders kept us from confronting our own problems, which is a real possibility. Goodness knows, if that were true, imagine how many of our own problems really needed attention. I can't imagine what it would have been like if we had been much more introspective. It probably saved us all to have the diversion.

Those were the heavy, introspective years. All the years seemed to have a lot of introspection, but some were more intense than others. I always thought that we learned so much from each person; each human being was such a gift.

Steve, a high school student, was very bright and had a high energy level. His intellect and ideas definitely enriched our lives. Edith, an author and our high school English teacher, with her strong intellect and patient presence, allowed Steve to see the writer in himself. Excellent with words and a keen observer, Edith deftly lead him to paper and pen.

His honest struggle, and even his not-so-honest struggle, in finding his way, enhanced our daily dramas and helped me to discover what was important. And what was important? To love, to include all, and to have the discipline to do it.

David, another live-in high school student, was contemplative and quiet. He discovered the artist in himself with the help of Kate Torres, a most remarkable art teacher. Not only could Kate teach people to draw and sculpt, but her open heart and interest in her students, combined with a hard-nosed drive for focus and excellence, gave each student unparalleled support for his abilities. David's discovery of himself through art wasn't an easy process, but it was exciting to be a part of and to witness the unfolding of his talent. These students were amazing. Certainly they were conflicted. But who wasn't? And who isn't? We all gained from each other, for which I am very grateful.

Another family that opened their home to many people was the Whitehouses. Brooks and Carol Whitehouse gave us great energy with the high school. Brooks worked in Boston each day and Carol took care of the kids. They became involved with The Well the same year the high school opened. They enrolled their son in the third grade at the start of school in the fall. By January, they had all four of their own children enrolled in our school and had "tuitioned" a fifth student who became a part of their family as well. Eventually, another high school student moved in with them also.

Carol could be seen in her suburban type car, ferrying six kids to school. With lunches in hand and book bags strategically stacked, all the kids would exit the car, tugging and hauling cellos, guitars, flutes, and skis. The older kids delivered the younger ones to their classrooms first, then they returned to the car for their own possessions.

During the ides of any month, Brooks could be found at his kitchen table paying bills with cotton in his ears to muffle the din of six different required instruments being practiced simultaneously. There were drawbacks to some of our curriculum!

Still, things weren't as cohesive as they might have been among the high school students and faculty. When a group of high school students felt rejected and unwanted by some of the faculty, Brooks was there ready to help. A few teachers had come to the conclusion that these students lacked the background to do high school work. Some of the students had gaps in their academic careers, but our emphasis had always been on willingness and effort. The gaps would close as the confidence rose. There were other teachers who felt that these students contributed value and life to the community, and they were willing to spend the time needed to fill in the gaps.

The faculty were of two opinions about which type of student should attend The Well. Because of the split that had developed between a group of high school students and some faculty, Brooks suggested that the high school students, faculty, and parents go on a retreat together. He knew a group facilitator who would help us mend the rift. Here's the bonus. "I'll pay for it," he told us as he flashed his broad, handsome smile. Peter, Jay's brother said, "This guy is too good to be true." He was true though, and he has remained so to this day.

The retreat was a remarkable experience. It was held in the Timber Doodle Hunting Lodge located in a neighboring town. The lodge had a huge wood-paneled room with a cathedral ceiling and exposed pine-log beams. The group leader presented activities that inspired trust, and at the end of each activity, everyone could discuss their thoughts and feelings that were elicited during the adventure. This was the first time I had ever been involved with anything like this, and I found it fascinating, frightening, and very instructive. So much information came out of spending a weekend together. Trust was the big issue; it was fascinating how little we all trusted each other. It was even more interesting to understand how lack of trust and openness can sabotage a community. Today these retreats and workshops are a part of the workplace, but thirty-two years ago, they were regarded as suspect by the uninitiated.

As for bringing the high school together, it didn't. Several of the students and faculty chose not to be a part of the weekend. Although it helped the individuals who did attend, the existing chasm in the school deepened, creating two groups that moved separately.

The high school program created high energy, lots of learning, and

He who does not trust enough, will not be trusted.
Lao-tse

great excitement. During those years, we started our chorus, lead by Jocelyn Bolle, who was and is, a wonderful musician. She also taught German in the high school. The second year of the high school, she offered to take her five second-year German students to Germany for spring vacation. They needed to raise funds for the trip. None of the students could afford it, but someone had the idea to have a Christmas Fair to raise money.

Earlier in the fall, a couple from Acworth had spent two days teaching us all how to macramé. There were strings tied to table legs, chairs or couches, and even to door knobs. (Occasionally, this caused a disaster when the vacuum came near and caught a string and wrapped it, along with the rest of the work, tightly around the rotary brush of the vacuum. Tears and endless unwinding followed.) From then on, at recess and lunch, students sat and tied knots together. Christmas Fair projects emerged everywhere—wall hangings, flowerpot hangers, belts, guitar straps, and table-runners. If students weren't doing macramé, they were weaving incredible inkle loom belts or knitting scarves.

I remember Jimmy teasing Aaron about his knitting, and I heard Aaron explaining to him that the activity organized the brain and improved reading skills. Jim's mother got wind of the information and the next day all of her boys were knitting. Class meetings and All School Meetings were hand-work workshops as well. The whole school made crafts for that first fair.

The Upper School, grades five through eight, always had three weeks of craft projects in December, so great leather crafts, batik items, woven goods, wall hangings, plant holders, woodwork products produced in Tony Brown's carpentry class, chairs, garden baskets, and matted drawings were constantly in the works. Faculty and parents contributed handcrafted items and baked goods. Students made wreaths and cut Christmas trees. Children worked as cashiers, sold pony rides, made popcorn balls, and sold popcorn and hot dogs. Students volunteered their services for full or half days of work. Some were auctioned as slaves to school parents to babysit, clean, or do lawn work. It was inspiring to have the fair student run. They must have been having fun, because nobody went home. Almost everybody from school was there each day of the fair from Friday night to Sunday afternoon.

Kate Torres, the art teacher, decorated the fair and artistically displayed the crafts and made the building come alive with her gift of design. She and I were a little bleary-eyed from burning the midnight oil the week before while trying to finish up miniature stables and barns for all the plastic model horses that were the rage in those days. When everything was set up, it looked magical. The glitter of the Christmas lights made the crafts look particularly beautiful in the evening. Freshly

*The stockings were hung by the chimney with care,
In hopes that St. Nicholas soon would be there.*
Clement C. Moore

cut spruce trees and evergreen wreaths spread their fragrance throughout the building. Everybody felt the magic, the electricity of it all.

Saturday night was a repeat story, but now the making of money added its own energy. The cashiers constantly totaled their hoard. We did raise enough money to send the students off to Germany in the spring. It was incredible that so many people worked so hard on behalf of a handful of students, especially when they had nothing to gain personally. Because everybody was so excited about working together for a common cause, the Christmas fairs were evermore devoted to a special cause each year, such as Operation Santa Claus or scholarships.

Part of the reason for the handsome monetary return was Ursula, everybody's "Oma," who came each day and bought many student-made crafts which she then displayed in her home for years. "Here comes Oma," the whisper would circulate throughout the building after a student had spied her little Volkswagon whipping up the driveway. Excitedly, the students watched her admire their work, wondering if theirs would be purchased. Would it be a gingerbread house, skillfully decorated by Jo and Tash? How about the batik rooster by Kambrah? "Brooks, she's buying your seagull!" Or Tara's macramé wall hanging? Ursula looked at each thing with such awe and touched each craft with such reverence; I knew it wasn't lost on the students.

Of course, she also put her money where her mouth was, and that fact wasn't lost on them either.

Ursula died in the spring of 2002, having been the ultimate grandmother for at least forty-five years and the ultimate school grandmother for thirty-four. While cleaning out the attic in her house, I found many of the children's crafts, each wrapped carefully. I set them to one side, planning to return them to their creators.

The trip to Germany was a success. For some of the students, it was their first time out of New England. In fact, some of the kids had never been as far as Boston before they came to The Well. How brave they all were to go. How wonderful to have a teacher like Jocelyn, who had the perseverance and imagination to bring it to fruition.

In the early Well years, all students were required to study an instrument. Everyone played the recorder in a group, but each had to learn to play an additional instrument of their choice. Piano and guitar were the most popular, but violin, cello, and flute lessons were also offered during school time. As a result, students missed one or more academic classes a week. They were expected to find out what class information they had missed and then get the homework from other students in the class.

We frequently had music programs in the afternoon. Early on, we realized that preparation for performances accelerated learning and created precious enthusiasm. Because there was so much music at The Well, Jay, Widdie (now the French teacher), Jonathan (Widdie's husband and English and guitar teacher), and I decided to have two musical venues. The daytime music program included piano, violin, and cello; the nighttime program, guitar, recorder, and flute. Of course, students could perform in either or both venues, depending on what was convenient for their parents.

Widdie and I thought it would be fun for the students to have a Coffeehouse for their parents. It would be a great format for the guitar students to perform their music. A mini-restaurant, how exciting! We asked the students if they would be interested in running a Coffee-house, with our help. The kids were really enthusiastic. We were off and running. The Coffeehouse would provide an evening of music for the parents. Students would prepare sandwiches and dessert and then serve food throughout the program. The idea was to create a warm, relaxed, and cozy atmosphere, with candles, small tables, and yummy things to eat. Chess would be offered for the quietly intelligent. Most of the students played chess; it was a very popular game at The Well. The carpeted stage provided an area for little ones to stretch out and listen. Small tables were needed.

Problem! There was no money in the budget for the tables. Widdie had the idea to gather huge, empty, wooden, telephone-cable spools that she had seen all over the countryside. We planned to take them apart, decorate and refinish them, and transform them into tabletops. One of the parents, by fluke, had a number of huge ice-cream bar-rels that were just the right height. We used them as pedestals for the spool tops. Eye hooks held the tops in place. It was no trouble get-ting enough spools; in fact, the telephone company gave us some. We found others on the side of the road.

The furnace room and downstairs art room became a sweatshop. We discovered Liquid Wrench. It was right up there as a miracle cure for rust. Each spool was held together with two or three long bolts and nuts, both mightily rusted from being exposed to the weather. After the spools were taken apart, they were sanded with a belt-sander, then hand sanded. Some of the kids stayed after school to work on the tables. Certain kids, like Ned, just wouldn't quit. They were dedicated and hardworking. When the sanding was done, the circular groove in the spool top where the drum had been set in was decorated and filled with tiles, pennies, or wood chips. The final step was three coats of Zip Guard, a polyurethane finish. I think we made about twelve or fifteen tables for that first Coffeehouse.

The date of the event arrived. Friday night. In those days, we had to clear everything out of the big classroom (sometimes referred to as

The Ballroom) for special events, so out went the cordwood that was lined along the wall, moved by a human chain of children. In came the ice-cream barrels and up went the new tabletops, glistening with their polyurethane sheen and tile and wood insets. Each person proudly showed the ones he or she had worked on. The next step was to set up the sound system. Then, turn the bathroom into a kitchen: Cut a hole in a piece of plywood, set it on a brace of two by fours over the tub, inset a stainless steel sink, run a black plastic hose from the tub spigot up through the plywood as a water source for the sink, and place a dish drain on the plywood counter. Place some boards above the sink for shelves. Voilá! A kitchen. Not quite—but close enough.

Since we had no supplies or dishes at the Upper Building, everything, and I mean everything, had to be brought up from our house, not very far away, but far enough to require a vehicle for convenience. Kambrah, Ak, and their friends seemed delighted to transport things in our Volkswagon. They got to drive, which enhanced the toting. Later, we used an old Ford truck to haul supplies back and forth.

The menu: The kids made roast beef sandwiches and Ukranian Coffee (coffee, whipped cream and honey, topped with an Eight o'Clock chocolate mint), served in tall glasses. There were delicious desserts—cream puffs, cakes, and cookies—made by students and parents. They served several kinds of tea, hot and cold cider, apples and oranges. Students were dishwashers, wait-people, bus-people, fruit sellers, and cashiers. The adults helped out, but the students wanted the primary responsibility of running the Coffeehouse as a special evening for their parents.

The girls all wore long madras or calico Gunni-sax floor-length dresses with hiking boots, usually Tyroleans, a unique combination. It was jeans and nice shirts for the boys. I can still see Cilla, a little first-grader, barefooted in her long, red-and-green plaid dress with white lace trim. Her large brown eyes were filled with concentration trying not to spill a drop (she didn't) or trip on her long dress as she delivered a cup of hot brew to her folks' table.

That first Coffeehouse was a Marx Brothers scene. There were no clear procedures. The mikes needed constant attention, and the guitars needed constant tuning and retuning, but the atmosphere was, nevertheless, electric.

Students sat on the stage and listened to the music, as they leaned comfortably against each other and joined in for the chorus. All of us sang, at times to support a timid musician. Occassionally the kitchen crew had to be warned of making too much noise: " Shhhhhhh!"

"Come on! Listen! Caleb's playing." Kids rushed from the kitchen to join the audience.

Kambrah and Kate played "Yankee Lady" and beautiful, clear sounds filled the room. Ak and Lisa harmonized. "I said the black bird...I will tell you the reason that" came over the mike. Young voices were singing together in harmony, lifting us, giving us only an inkling of true human potential but encouraging us to look for more.

And it's all such a delicate balance
The sport of infinity turns
And within every minute and space that is in it
Some how there is a beautiful face.

Every Coffeehouse offered some truly exceptional music. Liz's beautiful voice was sweet and clear as she sang "Bo Jangles." All of us wept and laughed as the sounds of Caleb's "Rainy Day People," a recorder groups' Telemann, and Kambrah and Sarah's delightful Scott Joplin tune filled the room. Babies and little ones were asleep on the stage or nestled in their brothers' and sisters' laps. In the candlelight, there were quiet chess games at the side tables. Jonathan lead the closing with, "A Gift to be Simple" or "Delicate Balance." All of us sang our hearts out. Our hearts were opened.

Fot that first Coffeehouse, I don't think we finished cleaning up until midnight. We had not anticipated that a line of adult friends and guest performers would be waiting in the wings for their chance to perform. Once on stage, they were reluctant to give up the limelight. When they did finish, hours later, the audience was bleary-eyed and close to sleep.

The firewood would have to be restacked on Monday, before school. There were many kinks to be worked out, but the students knew they had pulled off a wonderful evening.

The system didn't get refined. The fact is, we got a system. The kids made calligraphied menus, order pads and performance programs. Students signed up for jobs during the class meeting before each Coffeehouse date: dishwashers, kitchen and set up crew, guitar tuners, waiters, bus-boys, bakers, hot and cold drink servers. It became traditional for Jay's seventh-and-eighth graders to arrange the Ballroom. They moved cord wood, wheeled out the spool-top tables, hooked the ice-cream barrels in place, washed the kitchen area, and set up the sound equipment Friday afternoon before each Coffeehouse. When everything was set up the after- school crew loved to practice using the mikes; that became the bonus for helping out.

The pride the students derived from entertaining their parents inspired a lot of very fine music. The contact and warmth that was generated among the parents, faculty, and students added a new dimension to the school, bringing parents, students, teachers, and friends together in a social setting.

After twenty-five years or so, we lowered our standards and started using some paper products, making kitchen set-up and clean-up much faster. Things whipped right along in terms of organization, but the service never changed. It was always slow and inefficient; that was the price we paid for having children run it.

The price of teaching children to do everyday jobs and chores involves inefficiency for a while. Take "job-time," for instance. At the end of every school day, each student at The Well had a job that lasted between fifteen or twenty minutes. (The barn people took longer at times, but that was the allotted time.) Classes ended at 3:00 and jobs continued until 3:20. The students and faculty cleaned and organized the whole campus for the first thirty years. The last four years we hired someone part-time to help with the maintenance. Jay always plowed; later, Ak joined in, but everybody shoveled and sanded. The kids shoveled the roofs; removed snow from the pond with snow-blowers and ice scrapers; mowed lawns and cleared brush; cleaned the bathrooms,

Let chaos storm!
Let cloud shapes swarm!
I wait for form.
Robert Frost

the class rooms, and the halls; ordered supplies; and did yard work. Of course, the faculty worked right along with them. We all were needed to maintain our school and care for our environment. All of this took time to teach and learn.

Not only did the students become competent in all kinds of different jobs, but they developed a respect for their environment that was unconsciously high. I say unconsciously because they weren't aware that writing graffiti, or marring of property occurs regularly in school buildings. Just as it did not occur to them to write on their living-room wall at home, it never occurred to them to deface school property. They were remarkably conscious, however, in observing what needed to be done and great at doing it. Parents caught their spirit. Some would drop their plows on the way through, helping to clear the road of snow. At the end of special events, everybody—students, parents and teachers—worked to put things back in order.

Elliott Dacher, M.D. author of *Whole Healing and Intentional Healing*, discusses how helplessness weakens our immune system and renders people susceptible to disease. We always felt it was important for people to know how to actively take care of themselves and each other, to learn how things work, and to learn how to do things in order to be empowered themselves.

Working together to maintain the environment allowed children to gain real-life skills, skills that at a later age are much harder to acquire. To learn practical skills as an adult takes time, just as it does with any beginner. Generally, the adult opts out, pretending the job is beneath him. Eventually he believes that to be true and remains ignorant, dependent and helpless.

We were old-fashioned in believing that young children who learn to take care of themselves and to help others, develop common sense and become competent and self-confident adults. Giving children the experience of taking care of their environment and being empowered by the competence that creates is worth the time it takes and the hassle it involves.

The need for imagination, a sense of truth and a feeling of responsibility—these are the three forces which are the very nerve of education.
Rudolf Steiner

Sarah, long after she had left The Well was telling her college classmates about the plays she had done in a small school that she had attended. She described how much fun it was to set up and heat up dinner, pour drinks and fix bread and salad, for the twenty-five or thirty people at play rehearsal. She described the cozy candle-lit atmosphere the kids created for the actors, director, and lighting and sound crews. She noticed her friends looking at each other as if she had slipped a cog. "What?" she said. "What?" She knew she was suddenly treading in what others thought was the realm of the fantastic.

"You really did this?" her classmates inquired in disbelief.

"Did what?" she answered, a little defensively.

"You did the dinner, without adult help?"

"Well...four or five other kids helped too," she admitted. Until that moment, Sarah told us, she had never thought that there was anything unusual about the meal preparation. It had just been what the kids did and looked forward to doing. It's not the feeling of competence that holds so much power. Usually you don't even notice your own abilities. One takes them for granted. It's the feeling of incompetence that wields the force. Incompetence can be deadly.

The Well High School lasted two years. By the spring of the second year, the division between the faculty became too deep a chasm to bridge. One of the Well's basic tenets , inclusion, was sorely tested. The retreat didn't do the job we had hoped. At the time, the division among the faculty and students seemed unresolvable. Jay made the unbearably painful decision to discontinue the high school at the end of the second year, leaving the dissenting faculty free to form another school. It broke Jay's heart and the heart of many of the high school students who had put so much energy into it.

We were a little uneasy, that spring, as our seniors applied to colleges. We had elected not to be accredited since accreditation dictated the course selection, and we wanted the freedom for the teachers to teach what they knew and loved best. The seniors that graduated that year did gain entrance to the colleges of their choice: the State University of New York at New Paltz , Boston University, Harvard (two students) and an art school in Europe. The five graduates left and there were fifteen students who needed to find another high school. It proved that accreditation was not necessary for the next educational step.

The closing of the high school was devastating for us, particularly for Jay. When I think of the high school years, they remind me of the play *Godspell*. As in the play, the Well high school years contained the same wonderful, zany, off-the-wall student energy. People were searching for meaning, looking for their strengths, and often recognizing strengths in each other. The students developed close friendships through wonderful music, incredible art, and amazing poetry, and they discovered talents in everyone. Finally, the closing of the high school was a reminder of our failure to fulfill our intentions. It was a reminder of our inability to "stay awake," our failure to make inclusion work. However, grades kindergarten through nine did continue, and the school, a great deal richer for having had our experience with the high school, moved ahead. *Godspell* was to become one of our favorite Well productions.

In 1971, Ruth Pitman, an art teacher, came to The Well and she was to have a profound effect on everyone she taught. She truly saw the artist in every student, and she magically drew it forth. A fine artist and craftswoman, she inspired us all. The children used paint, clay, and block-prints to illustrate what they were reading in class. They made incredible black and white linoleum prints of *The Bible*, which I always thought should be published in a book. Rich in the artistic and Anthroposophical background, Ruth brought the radiant use of color to The Well. More importantly, she possessed a gentle, intuitive understanding of each child and an ability to provide the help each needed. Art was always allotted the same importance as other subjects

Only through art con we emerge from ourselves and know what another person sees.

Marcel Proust

at The Well, so students had three to four hours of instruction a week. Our dictum was be in touch with and to create beauty daily in order to give balance to each day. The Well was constantly blessed with faculty members who had remarkable talent and encouraged those moments for their students.

That year Carol began teaching at The Well, as she has often said, "with her vacuum cleaner." She helped me clean the classrooms with the students. She helped with math, reading, and all other areas during the day, sharing her expertise and humor. She had been an active parent at The Well for two years before she entered the classroom. Our children were friends and were all about the same ages. She had tremendous energy, a great sense of humor, and a wonderful appreciation for children. A woman of quick wit, she could make anything fun. She didn't last very long, however, in my classroom, much to my disappointment. The Upper Building needed a math and reading teacher. I was reluctant to give her up, but martyr that I am, I did. Carol, with her energy, love of learning, and her love of people, graced The Well for the next twenty years,.

Our families grew up side by side. We shared so many joys and we shared our sorrows. Together we discovered some of the many faces of ourselves, some joyous, some painful to behold; we created a lasting friendship built on gratitude and love. We learned to open our hearts together. We saw our flaws and we still felt loved. Working and playing together with our children and our husbands enriched us both.

I grew up with brothers and felt lucky to have them. I never wanted a sister until I met Carol, when I realized what I had missed in not having had one. Fortunately, she became an integral part of my life development, of all of ours. I always thought that Carol was one of the bravest people I ever knew. We might be together doing something daring—skiing in the most inclement weather with howling winds and blowing snow; hammering siding onto a barn wall, our extension ladders swaying in the breeze; playing all-out ice hockey, both laugh-

Whatever thing men call great, look for it in Joan of Arc, and there you will find it.
Mark Twain

ing and having a great time—but we would both be a little giddy from the adrenalin. And why do I think she was brave? Because she foresaw all the dangers, took them into account, and did what she wanted anyway. I just did it impulsively, simply seeing the goal and enjoying the journey. I never knew anyone more intelligent or more loving. Carol lived the adage, "Be true to yourself."

The children were loved and nourished by so many adults. This was one of the best aspects of The Well. Seldom is there a setting where so many people want the best for each other and are willing to do what it takes to help them achieve it. Parents cheered and clapped not only for their own children, but for all children. Noticing and acknowledging progress in your own child is great. Noticing and acknowledging growth and development in other people's children is a blessing, something that lifts the whole community and allows it to breathe. The support for all was a part of daily life at school and spread from parent to teacher to child and back to parent, completing the circle. The force of love, combined with explicit approval, has to be the best atmosphere for living and learning.

The years of the energy crisis took place in the '70s so more wood stoves came into many houses in New Hampshire. Most fall weekends were devoted to accumulating wood or felling trees for the next year's supply. Families got together to make the job more fun and to have the process go a little faster. The kids were a tremendous help in the wood-lines, passing the logs along. Brooks called them the "army of ants" and they were that effective. We hauled, cut, and split cord-upon-cord of wood. Much of New Hampshire did. Wood Day, in those days, was totally about wood and the clearing of woods. The agenda of Wood Day broadened as the need to clear land and burn wood subsided. Gardening and bulb planting, accompanied by hot drinks and bagels, snuck in as wood lost its priority, but for the first twenty-five years, it was wood. On Wood Day at the Well, trucks arrived—some dragging

Courage is the resistance to fear, mastery of fear, not the absence of fear.
Mark Twain

A new commandment I give unto you, that ye love one another...By this shall all men know that ye are my disciples, if ye have love for one another.
John 13:34-35

*We dance around the
ring and suppose,
The secret sits in the
middle and knows.*
Robert Frost

a wood-splitter—bearing kids, chain-saws, axes, and wedges. Everyone worked to cut, haul, split and stack wood. Kids rode on trailers and trucks they had helped pile high with wood. Brush was stacked for burning later when the snow came. Around noon, everything stopped, and a wild parent versus student soccer game started that lasted until we were all covered in mud and sweat. We ended the day with a brown bag picnic. At the close of every Wood Day, I always let out a long sigh of relief, glad that so much had been accomplished and thankful that we all still had our fingers and toes and no broken bones. After Wood Day, many of us did need Sunday afternoon to lie on the couch to rest our aching muscles or to stretch out on the floor to straighten our slightly askew backs.

During the first five years, many traditions or programs became established both in our own family and the school family. A tradition in our home was singing grace before dinner, so at all Well dinners we sang a round twice through and ended with the rousing line, OUR FATHER IN HEAVEN. I had a picture of God sitting up in heaven, listening with his hands over ears as we approached the final phrase. The mental image always makes me smile. Nonetheless, acknowledged gratitude is the best attitude. Giving and receiving is what keeps it all going.

Many activities that were introduced that first year became cherished traditions: Eskimo baseball, played in the field or at the beach; family days at the ocean on Plum Island; Wood Day; soccer and ice hockey (all ages); parent conferences, some endless, with the whole family; Shakespeare (and other wonderful) plays; play rehearsal suppers; kids star-gazing; brush burning; wood lines and stacking wood; sanding the driveway; coming to school, regardless of the weather; the Peter Garland kids arriving at school on horseback; daily journals filled with what are now childhood memories; writing books; reading the classics, the Greeks and the Romans, myths and fairytales; hiking, trips up Mt. Skatutakee; more overnights under the stars; Coffeehous-

*If you don't stand for
something, you'll fall
for anything.*
Unknown

es and music programs; poetry recitals; parents and teachers working, playing, learning and growing together. Failing and trying again. These traditions were established early on.

A community tradition involved parents and teachers sitting around the dining-room table discussing everything: children, students, marriage, spirituality, politics, curriculum, higher-selves, lower-selves, middle-selves, values, honesty, truth, new teaching methods. Some discussions were fraught with strong emotions, but the force of love sorted a lot out and the rest...the rest we gave to the Universe to work out. In the early days, this often took place in a smoke filled room. The air cleared as we got older, in more ways than one.

Job time, play rehearsal, overnights, and cleaning up after breakfast while listening to the Hallelujah Chorus. Contra dancing with Dudley's fiddle—all this as well as the day-to-day, ordinary routines became the foundation for years to come. Jay and I felt it was a tremendous privilege to share all of this with our own children; we were lucky to be surrounded by such a vibrant community. It gave us the opportunity to learn how to construct buildings, tend a garden, care for animals, and most of all, to examine

I remember...

Staying after school for play rehearsals, holding study halls in the big classroom with an ear cocked toward the stage in case Jay called my name to rehearse, having big group dinners at the Brick Building, bunking down on every available flat surface and giggling until late at night, and playing loud classical music during clean up the next morning

When those overnights ended and I was the only one who stayed over since I lived so far away. And one night when Jay drove everyone home after rehearsal, including me, even though I lived so far away.

Discussing smoking cessation with Toni and her comparing it to a candy addiction. She was right, it was impossible to stop eating candy altogether.

Feeding the horses and learning from the older kids how to do all the 'jobs'. And learning how to vacuum from Jay.

Writing conferences, how scary and how wonderful to be saddled with the expectations and undivided attention of someone else's parent, pitying the poor person who got MY mother.

Spending history class scraping the pond for ice skating, the wars between the figure and hockey skaters, the wonderful moment when I managed to do something constructive with a hockey stick and got praise from Jay or Ak.

All school singing classes/operetta rehearsals with Jocelyn Bolle at the piano and Jay and Carol singing right along with everyone else. Poetry recitals and competition with Tina Brown to find the longest, most interesting story poem (Roald Dahl's "Goldie Pinklesweet," Robert Service's "The Shooting of Dan McGrew," and "The Cremation of Sam McGee".)

Stacking wood, passing logs from arm to arm, and worrying about falling stacks and gangrenous mushrooms.

Geography lesson and speed tests pointing to capitals on a map or globe. Learning postal abbreviations (I still remember them!)

History classes when we were alternately cursed (by classmates) and praised (by Jay) for asking good questions.

"Waitressing" at coffee houses, making block prints with Mrs. Pittman, project weeks, "jumps" courses in the woods, burying flower bulbs in random places, and garbage collection by the pound.

Melissa Herman (class of '81)

our hearts on a regular basis, and to teach and raise our children in a life that we loved. Our children learned to read, write and explore math with us and with their friends. The first five years of The Well established a great deal for us as a family. We were discovering our values, sorting out the truths from all the things that held some truth. We truly were lucky; only much later was I to realize that we were truly blessed.

ODE TO THE WELL

"I think that I shall never see
A poem lovely as a ....

Treat you to a memory you say?
And so I shall, without delay.

Kids of all kinds-some headstrong, some shy,
Some serious, some funny, some clever, some wry.

There were goats and sheep and chickens (quite tasty),
And a couple of geese who, I'm afraid, were quite nasty.

Kasha, Champion, Lucky, and Penny,
And a pickle-loving donkey called Jennie.

A ram named Bill with a bit of a problem
That involved taking aim at unsuspecting bottoms!

Camel and Hamish and Bobtail, too,
Bunnies and guinea pigs, to name a few.
Katie, Carol, Sally, Billie, and Libby,
Ruth, Jocelyn, Jonathan, Gundi, and Widdy.

Parents and teachers, one and the same—
Kept us students at the top of our game.

Fields and streams cleared by one and all,
And bonfires burning orange and tall.

Riding at the Williams just up the road,
John Kulish's lessons about bear, tree and toad.

Soccer, red rover-and in all of these years,
I've learned Eskimo baseball is only played HERE!

The construction of dams in the mud-season driveway
Turning parental pick-ups into a big pothole highway.

Woods lull of tree forts and obstacle courses,
And a village of Peeps that grew quite enormous.

Renaissance fairs long before they were trendy,
And a Christmas Fair that was quite dandy.

Chasing runaway ponies up from the Achilles',
Or climbing the brambles of Mt. Skatutakee.

Field trips to Plum Island, the Museum of Fine Arts,
The Boston Aquarium-you parents were nuts!

From "See Spot Run." And "Little Bear,"
To Aesop and Grimm, Shakespeare and Moliere.

Queen Nefertiti, Caesar, and Greece;
Jason, Odysseus, and the Golden Fleece.

Wordly wise, project weeks, times tables.
Poetry Days, quiet time, and cubbyholes.

In school and class meetings we learned to speak up
And accept praise and criticism with equal aplomb.

Play rehearsals that ran late into the night,
While scenery was painted on muslin pulled tight.

Costumes and makeup and learning of lines;
Songs to be sung at the appropriate time.

Romeo? Where's Romeo? Someone call Ondine.
Androcles, Androcles: It's time for your scene.

Has there ever been in the history of plays,
A director more patient or generous than Jay?

Or the magical culinary powers of Toni,
Who could feed millions with mere macaroni?

Parents sitting 'round the huge kitchen table,
Catching up on stories whenever they were able.

The electric atmosphere of coffeehouse night:
Bavarian coffees in the music-filled candlelight.

"Catch as Catch Can," and "me-ee-ee-a-ow,"
Recorders, guitars, piano, flutes, and cello.

And I can't help but mention a notable crash
Involving a fish tank, salamanders, and broken glass.

But what's hard to explain-so hard to express-
Is the magic of this school that was its behest.

Just try to describe to someone not familiar,
And they can't understand a place so peculiar

That the children have opinions and the classics are fresh.
Where both art and science inform the process.

They tend to look quizzical, like you made it all up.
As if Hogwarts were real, or Middle Earth just dug up!

But most remarkable of all, a family opened a school
That became a family with an ever-widening pool.

So what have we learned, what does it all mean?
When the Hallelujah chorus plays, it's time to clean.

Tad Wilson

SOURCES

101 Great American Poems, (New York: Dover, 1998)

The Book of the It, Georg Groddeck, (New York: International Universities Press, 1976)

Buddha's Little Instruction Book, Jack Kornfield (New York: Bantam Books 1994

Celebrating My Teacher, (Heartfelt Samplers, Inc 1992)

Classic Poems to Read Aloud, selected by James Berry, (New York: Kingfisher, 1995)

Collected Poems of Emily Dickinson Original editions edited by Mabel Loomis and T.W. Higginson. (New York: Gramercy Books, 1982)

The Essential Rumi, translated by (Coleman Barks San Francisco: Harper, 1995)

The Golden Treasury From Gifted Minds, compiled by Stella Hadley Hickman, (Baltimore, New York: Broadway Publishing Company, 1909)

Holy Bible, (Grand Rapids: Zondervan, 1994)

Immortal Poesm of the English Language, edited by Oscar Williams, (New York: Washington Square Press, Pocket Books, 1952)

Learning to Fall, Philip Simmonds (New York: Bantam Books, 2000)

Life Prayers From Around the World edited by Elizabeth Roberts and Elias Amidon (San Francisco: Harper, 1996)

Proverbs For Daily Living, Complied by John P. Beilenson (White Plains:The Peter Pauper Press, 1992)

Quips and Quotes edited by Evan Esar (New York: Doubleday, 1968)

Small Miracles II by Yitta Halberstam Mandelbaum and Judith Leventhal (Holbrook Mass: Adams Media Corporation, 1998)

Tao Te Ching by Lao Tsu translated by Gia Fu Feng and Jane English (New York: Vintage books, 1972)

The Way of the Sufi by Idries Shah (London: Penguin Group, 1968)

Webster's Treasury of Relevant Quotations, Edward F. Murphy, (New York: Greenwich House, 1983)

Book Design by Sarah Bauhan and Henry James
Type set in Monotype Centaur and Fred Smeijers FF Quadraat
Printed in Canada by Transcontinental Printing